Jeremiah 29:11 The Plans I Have For You Man: Be Champions!

Written by: Dr. Brandi DeShawn Brown
Edited by: Courtney Berry, Chief Editor Iron Proof Editing.

By: Dr. Brandi DeShawn Brown

Edited by: Courtney Berry

ISBN 978-0-9896965-2-4

School Street School-Counseling and Consulting Services
Rockford, Illinois 61101

Book Cover Illustration by Janessa Wilkins

Contents

Dedication

To: My Champions,

Son:	Carandus Brown, Jr.
Fathers:	George Briggs Bacon II
	John Devereueawax
Grandfathers:	George Briggs Bacon, Sr.
	Jim Johnson
Great-Uncle:	Harold Johnson
Brothers:	Andre, Johnny, & Jonathan

My Uncles:
Victor, 'JJ' John, Jimmy, Bart, Harold Jr., Ronnie, Tommy, Charles, Bill

My Nephews:
Jahmeir, Julius, Jonathan Jr., Kylan

You are my champions!! I love you all!

Acknowledgements

Courtney Berry, I'm thankful for your writing and editing gifts. Thank you for your editing expertise in these writing projects. You are a blessing!

Charlyne Blatcher-Martin, Thank you for consulting ideas and making edits in the beginning stages of these books. I'm grateful for all your services!

Penny Devereueawax, Thank you for spiritual support in the stages and development of these books. I'm thankful for all your support!

Domonique S. Devereueawax for early editing. Thank you Sis!

Antar Baker and Rev. Chester and Mrs. Doris Baker family for spiritual and educational consulting during this writing journey.

Imani Brown and Jamaia Brown for assisting in these writing projects. Thank you for being faithful.

Pastor Charlene Bulls-Mills and Allen Chapel A.M.E. Church Rockford, IL. Thank you for all your support during this journey.

Introduction

The purposes of this book

    My prayer is that this book brings you the light and hope you need to prosper in the plans God has for you. This book is designed for you to find strength in the situation you are facing through the transitions of still point moments and reflections. The author encourages the reader to "keep the end in mind with a victory" and become desperate for God's promise, purpose, and plans for your life.

    Your social role as either a son, brother, husband, father, uncle, or community member is necessary for the Jeremiah 29:11 plans for you and someone else. You can help someone understand and develop into his or her Jeremiah 29:11 purposes with your social roles.

    Jeremiah was a prophet assigned to the Israelites. His message from God was simple. It was to turn to God. The Israelites did not listen to Jeremiah. One of the reasons was because of King Jehoiachin and other priests did not listen to God or Jeremiah. Israel was eventually invaded and captured by the Babylonians. While Jerusalem lived in Babylon's captivity, their leader, Evil-merodach was kind to King Jehoiachin (Jeremiah 52:31). For example, this king spoke pleasantly, gave preferential treatment over the other exiled kings in Babylon (32), replaced his prison garb and supplied him with new clothes and allowed him to sit at the king's table (33), and gave him a regular allowance to cover his living expense for the rest of his life (34).

    In these scriptures, hope for the fallen Jerusalem is revealed through kindness from an evil king. God will turn your enemies to be kind to you. Acts of kindness can give people going through a tough situation hope and confirmation to their prayer. Let me encourage you to have hope in your situation and not to fear your enemy. Pray and trust God right now! God will tell you what He wants you to do (James 1:5). All you have to do is ask.

    God has a message for you in the Word. You have to receive the Word or the message. The nation of Israelites was warned many times to turn away from sin. This generation sinned against God which led to their life of captivity in Babylon. They lost their homes, businesses, Solomon's Temple, and agriculture lands and farms established by previous generations. God sent warning to the Israelites before the invasion by the Babylonians. Before the exile, Jeremiah delivered many messages to the elders, priests, prophets, and all the people. One of the letters to these people read:

Jeremiah 29:4 The Lord Almighty, the God of Israel, sends this message to all the captives he has exiled to Babylon from Jerusalem: (5) Build homes, and plan to stay. Plant gardens, and eat the food you produce. (6) Marry, and have children. Then find spouses for them, and have many grandchildren. Multiply! Do not dwindle away! (7) And work for the peace and prosperity of Babylon. Pray to the Lord for that city where you are held captive for if Babylon has peace, so will you."

(8) The Lord Almighty, the God of Israel, says, "Do not let the prophets and mediums who are there in Babylon trick you. Do not listen to their dreams (9) because they prophesy lies in my name. I have not seen them," says the Lord. (10) The truth is that you will be in Babylon for seventy years. But then I will come and do for you all the good things I have promised, and I will bring you home again.

(11) For I know the plans I have for you," says the Lord. "They are plans for good and not for disaster, to give you a future and a hope. (12) In those days when you pray, I will listen. (13) If you look for me in earnest, you will find me when you seek me. (14) I will be found by you," says the Lord. "I will gather you out of the nations where I sent you and bring you home again to your own land."

This book, *"Jeremiah 29:11 The Plans I Have for You, Man: Be Champions,"* is designed for you to know that you have a promise according to the scripture Jeremiah 29:11.

Did you know that you have a promise? What is a promise? A promise is a declaration that someone will or will not do something for you. It is a vow; an indication of something to come. It is an indication of future excellence or success. John 1:1 and 2 Corinthians 1:20-22 reveal that your promise existed in the beginning and it can only come through knowing God.

The promise of God is the Word of God. *John 1: 1 In the beginning the Word already existed. He was with God, and He was God.*

Here's what God declared for you: *2 Corinthians 1:20 For all of God's promises have been fulfilled in Him. That is why we say "Amen" when we give glory to God through Christ. (21) It is God who gives us, along with you, the ability to stand firm for Christ. He has commissioned us, (22) and he has identified us as his own by placing the Holy Spirit in our hearts as the first installment of everything he will give us.*

Jeremiah 29:11 is the key scripture. Your promise is waiting for you to know your purpose. Therefore, it is time to make some transitions to receive the destiny in store for YOU. Our Heavenly Father promised that He will never leave us or forsake us. In the plans God has for you, it is an indication of something to come and of future excellence or success. The plans God has for you is to embrace a future with hope and prosperity with a Jeremiah 29:11 identity. Now is the time to make the transition to understand and mature into the Jeremiah 29:11 plans and purpose for you. Examining your seasons, people, and places can help you understand your present situations. In this process you need to have understanding and hope in the Jeremiah 29:11 plans God has for you.

Why change? You cannot afford to remain the way you are! Your purpose is waiting for a strategy to get you towards the Jeremiah 29:11 plans. You can bring your promise to permission with steps to align to your Jeremiah 29:11 plans and purposes. The process of change means that you will experience transition from one level to the next. In this practice you may experience separation from old things, places, and people. New connections will take place with new things, places, and people to a new season. God sets you seasons and times and you will mature from the old you to the new you.

Do you know your purpose? It is important to examine your situation and relationship with God and people because your promise determines where you are going to be. The people you've yoked with are critical to understanding your purpose. Your answer to understanding your purpose is in the Word of God and people listening to God.

What to do when you change? There are some things you can do while you are waiting for confirmation about your purpose. First, you have to change your mind-sets, pray about strongholds, forgive yourself and others, un-yoke yourself from relationships, and be still. In the meantime learn to wait on your promise by reading the Word of God. The Word of God will tell you what to do next if you'll be still and have an open spirit to accept. Second, it is important to keep your faith in God about your future. You will make transitions from glory-to-glory and faith-to-faith. It is important to keep your faith in God when you experience obstacles.

You are in a shift. As you read and discover your Jeremiah 29:11 seed, you will start to have hope in your future and start to prosper according to God's Will. In this transition, you will mature in Christ, and get loose from the people, places, and things you no longer needed in your next levels. You have to keep your eyes towards Heaven where all your help comes from (Psalm 121:1-2). Believe that you are in the right place and don't give up in your test.

The objective is to know that you have a promise while you are between old situations and your promise; and experience shifts, interruptions, and in your transition to your next level. As you continue to read:

1. You will learn that you have a promise according to Jeremiah 29:11.
2. Don't let other people take advantage of your promise. Evaluate your crowd. Your crowd will either crowd or crown you.
3. Evaluate the people who want to yoke with you. Evaluate any relationships/people's intention to either be a burden or answered prayer?

Man of God, the purpose of this book is to share with you Jeremiah's message that God has plans for you to have hope in your right now situations and future. Also, to encourage you to go through your situations like a champion. Jesus is your example of a champion because His realities came to pass. *Jeremiah 29:11 The Plans I Have For You Man: Be Champions* is an announcement of your future to have hope and faith in God. God's promises and hope is for you is to have peace in your situations. Be encouraged because you are built for your purpose to prosper and have victory.

God's Plan for Man: Prosper

Man of God, prosperity is in your future. You are creators and producers. Therefore, you have to continually pray and plant the Word of God into your households, spouse, children, and field placements. Break the ground with hope and faith in the word according to Hebrews 11:1. Get ready to plant the Word of God through Bible study, prayer and meditation time, and personal relationship with God.

God's Plan for Man: Plant

God gives seed to the sower. Be like a farmer that cares about their seed to receive a harvest. It's time to clean up and watch your ground, mature spiritually, and keep the end in mind according to Hebrews 11:1. *Luke 8:5-15 But the good soil represents honest, good-hearted people who hear God's message, cling to it, and steadily produce a huge harvest.* Take the time you need to cultivate the ground. Like a farmer, you have to pull up weeds, thorns, and rocks which will hinder your seed to sprout. Use this time to forgive yourself and others. Get to the root of your problem through forgiveness of self, reconcile relationships with others, and walk with a renewed spirit. You have to examine your ground on a daily basis to reap a harvest of joy, peace, self-control, and happiness.

Make time to watch over your ground for thorns and rocks. Birds and other insects and animals will come into your field only to dig up your seed or move your seed. Don't let the devil prowl around your field and try to steal your seed. Keep watch over the paths in your field to protect your harvest. While you wait for your harvest, you can read the Word of God, pray, and fast to understand the secrets of the Kingdom of God.

God's Plans for Man: Wait

While you wait, have great faith with the end in mind. This means keep in mind the vision God has shown you about your Jeremiah 29:11 purposes. Therefore, keep your vision in mind when you experience obstacles. God has given you the victory. It's going to rain, but God has you covered during your seasons. Begin to thank God in your secret place of praying for your children and the Kingdom treasures He has given you. Create your secrete place while you wait. *Psalm 91:1 Those who live in the shelter of the Most High will find rest in the shadow of the Almighty.* While you continue to wait, you need to sow into your harvest.

God's Plan for Man: Harvest

Continue to pull up weeds and allow God to remove the figs out of your field. God is in control of your seasons. Thank Him for spring buds, sprouts, and new growth in your field.

Matthew 21: (18) In the morning, as Jesus was returning to Jerusalem, he was hungry, (19) and he noticed a fig tree beside the road. He went over to see if there were any figs on it, but there were only leaves. The he said to it, "May you never bear fruit again!" And immediately the fig tree withered up. (20) The disciples were amazed when they saw this and asked, "How did the fig tree withered up. (21) Then Jesus told them, "I assure you, you can do things like this and much more. You can even say to this mountain, "May God lift you up and throw you into the sea, and it will happen. (22) If you believe, you will receive whatever you ask for in prayer."

The Jeremiah 29:11 plans God has for you were made and spoke out into existence from God. There is a command from the mouth of God, i.e. a word, a prophecy spoken over your life to prosper in God's Will. Thus, God is agricultural. God is a planter of seeds and He watches over them according to Isaiah 27:3 and Jeremiah 1:12. God has promised to watch over you when you have faith and walk in righteousness. You have a Jeremiah 29:11 seed within you that God is watching over, protecting, and guiding. Therefore, you need to have a relationship with God to understand and discover the plans God has for you.

As you read, let me encourage you to be like the farmer that seeks the Lord's wisdom, and plants the seeds of faith and treasures of the Word of God in your heart. Remember to remain connected in the vineyard's court and connected to the vine! Everything you need: your miracle, joy, peace, understanding, wisdom, love, happiness, and healing is in the Vineyard's court. My brothers, please pray with expectations as you grown into the Jeremiah 29:11 plans for you. God has a harvest in your field when you remain connected to Jesus, the True Vine. The seeds of God's Word will produce a harvest for you and your family to receive many blessings as you mature into your Jeremiah 29:11 identities.

Introduction of Still Points, Still Point Moments, and Still Point Reflections

The Word of God tells us to be silent and be still. Let me empower you with two still moment scriptures:

1. *Be silent, and know that I am God! I will be honored by every nation. I will be honored throughout the world* (Psalm 46:10)

2. *He that is unjust, let him be unjust still: and he which is filthy, let him be filthy still: and he that is righteous still: and he that is holy, let him be holy still* (Revelation 22:11).

God wants you to be still and silent and understand your Jeremiah 29:11 purposes. In the plans God has for you, God wants you to be still. As you read, you will come across **Still Point Scriptures, Moments, and Reflections** for devotional time. Each chapter will begin with still point scriptures and prayer to begin your section reflection. "Reflection" can mean to ponder, meditate, give back, or show an image. As you reflect on your still point moments be sure to meditate on the scriptures and God's purpose and plan. The word devote can mean to consecrate, dedicate, or to give up something. Devotion can mean to attach to a cause or person. God wants us to devote our time, that He has blessed us with, back to Him. Devotion is your one-on-one time with God. Devote time to be silent and still to hear the plans for you. Fellowship with God requires fellowship with the Lord to discover your purpose. Are you ready to follow God? There are many examples of people who followed Jesus in this book that devoted their ways, time, and life to living according to the Word. As you read the devotions, you should devote moments to reflect and have devotions on your Jeremiah 29:11 plans.

The end of each chapter will include **Still Point Reflections**. Reflection means to have deep thought or indirect approach. The still point reflection is your moment to have devotion, deep thought, and indirect approach to stay on the path God has prepared for you.

Still point scriptures, moments, and reflections are designed for you to examine your situation and give it to Jesus. Let's examine the scripture from Mark 4:38:-41.

(35) As evening came, Jesus said to his disciples, "Let's cross to the other side of the lake." (36) He was already in the boat, so they started out, leaving the crowds behind (although other boats followed). (37) But soon a fierce storm arose. High waves began to break into the boat until it was nearly full of water.

(38) Jesus was sleeping at the back of the boat with his head on a cushion. Frantically they woke him up, shouting. "Teacher, don't you even care that we are going to drown?" (39) When he woke up, he rebuked the wind and said to the water, "Quiet down!" Suddenly the wind stopped, and there was a great calm. (40) And he asked them, "Why are you so afraid? Do you still not have faith in me?" (41) And they were filled with awe and said among themselves, "Who is this man, that even the wind and waves obey him?"

God is the Father of time and our seasons; and He knows what we are going through. God wants us to have faith in Him no matter what the situation looks like or where we are going. The disciples witnessed Jesus *heal a man with a deformed hand (Mark 3:1). Also, Jesus and his disciples went out to the lake, followed by a huge crowd from all over Galilee, Judea (Mark 3:7), (8) Jerusalem, Idumea, from east of the Jordan River, and even from as far away as Tyre and Sidon.* The disciples and the crowds are witnesses of Jesus' miracles and teachings. Faith in God is the key when you experience challenges. God wants to do mighty works and miracles through those with great faith. Will you believe that God has plans for you? It is time to be still and silent to become wise faith walkers.

Still Point Moment

Have you ever been in a situation and asked God if He cared what you are going through? It is important to be still and understand that God is near. God has many promises that require you to have great faith. In order for you to gain and receive these promises, it is important to have a relationship with God the Father, Jesus the Son, and Holy Spirit, the comforter. The Trinity Team is near and on duty. Be still (pray) and silent (listen and look for God) in the storm. Don't lose your faith when your boat gets rocked.

Preface Still Point Reflection

You serve a God that is bigger than your circumstances and problems. Where is your faith? Faith in God will take you to your next level living. Faith in God will give you courage to live in your next level, face the next test, and go through your situation. If you began to experience obstacles, let me encourage you to have faith!

After Jesus calmed the winds and waves, the boat made it to the other side (Mark 5:1). As soon as the boat crossed the lake, Jesus healed a man in the land of the Gerasenes instantly (Mark 5:1-8). You are on your way to the next level of the Jeremiah 29:11 plans God has for you! Stay in the boat and keep your faith. Have courage to rebuke the raging winds and waves that rock your boat. You are on your way to the other side. Like the man instantly healed by Jesus, you have a blessing ready to change your life. Your faith will become a testimony to tell someone what wonderful things the Lord has done for you and how merciful He has been. Throughout this book, you will explore the plans God has for you by reading about men, husbands, and fathers from the Bible.

Section Summaries

Section One:
God's Plans for Man: Discover Your Jeremiah 29:11 Purpose

This section is to announce the Jeremiah 29:11 plans and purposes in your life. God's plan and purpose for men are to have dominion in the positions as sons, husbands to wives, brothers, cousins, uncles, and friends in their Ephesians 4:11 positions as apostles, prophets, evangelists, pastors, and teachers. The people you meet and have relationships with have a purpose for a season. You are gifted and wonderfully made by God. There is a process to understand the plans God has for you. In the process you become more faith-conscious of who you are in the dominion of your Jeremiah 29:11 identities.

Section Two
God's Plan for Man: Have Integrity

Show up for your meetings with God. Once you realize your purpose and vision, keep a good reputation. Know your purpose and don't allow people to stop or stand in the way of your purpose. People may not understand your purpose, but your gifts are in the hands of God. God is at work in your life. This means that you are in a safe place. Therefore, you need to know and recognize your season. It's important to know your Jeremiah 29:11 identities even when people don't receive you. Don't give up when people belittle who they think you are.

Section Three
God's Plans for Man: Have Faith

Your field has a purpose. You will experience a transformation as you see your Jeremiah 29:11 purpose and accept your assignment. Transformation in this text refers to a new lifestyle which includes repenting, changing, and opening your mind. Understand your past to face your future. Your past is your stepping stone to take you to your next level. The process you are experiencing has a purpose. You have been given charge of something; therefore, you have to have faith when facing difficulties, lies, and setbacks; always remember that the challenge is part of the process.

Section Four
God's Plans for Man: Be Champions

It is important to understand your strengths and weaknesses when you're on your Jeremiah 29:11 assignments. Don't allow your gifts to diminish when challenges take place. You've been given charge of your gifts and talents. The process you are experiencing in your field is designed to complete God's plan. God will bless you in your field. God is changing you; therefore, you don't have to explain yourself to others.

Section Five
God's Plans for Man: The Ministry of Fatherhood

Release your past to receive your future. Have a vision and mission for your family. You may have to be a male figure to someone that is fatherless, brotherless, or helpless. Understand your role as a mentor, teacher, coach, or advisor to the individual in their season(s) of discovering their Jeremiah 29:11 assignments and purposes.

Section Six
God's Plans for Man: Delegate Authority

Moses' new role, new location, new assignment in Sanai's valley and mountain included a plan and purpose for future generations. The people in your life have a purpose to advise you in the plans God has for you. As a man, you may have to delegate authority to the people assigned to you. Assigning tasks to others helps them develop skills and knowledge for their next levels. Most of all, delegating authority can help reduce stress and work-overload.

Section One:
Discover Your Jeremiah 29:11 Purpose

God's Plans for Man: Commit to Your Assignment

Look at your situation with an end view. This means look at every situation you go through as a victory. Victory and work are written in the Jeremiah 29:11 plans for you. The "Commit to Your Assignment," section is designed to empower you to have a faith walk. Faith without works is dead (James 2:14). Therefore, you have to work in your Jeremiah 29:11 assignments because your faith and vision will get challenged. Be encouraged as you read about commitment. The principles in commitment require you to work in your Jeremiah 29:11 assignments. The objective is to know that your faith has an assignment. As you continue to read, be still as you discover your Jeremiah 29:11 identities.

Still Point: *Commit yourself to instruction; attune your ears to hear words of knowledge (Proverbs 23:12).*

You will be tested as you discover the Jeremiah 29:11 plans God has for you. Let me encourage you with Proverbs 23:12: *Commit yourself to instruction; attune your ears to hear words of knowledge.* The Word of God is designed to comfort and give you strength in your Jeremiah 29:11 assignments. From the womb of God to His mouth, He formed the waters, land, plants, and animals. These creations are designed and commanded to bless, protect, and hide you. God wants you to keep on praying no matter what is taking place in your life. Therefore, you need to hear God's instructions to pass the tests that are before you.

(Genesis 2:8) *God created and made everything and planted a garden in Eden, in the east, and there He placed the man he had created. (9) And the Lord God planted all sorts of trees in the garden, beautiful trees that produced delicious fruit. At the center of the garden he placed the tree of life and the tree of the knowledge of good and evil. (15) The Lord God placed the man in the Garden of Eden to tend and care for it. (16) But the Lord God gave him this warning: "You may freely eat any fruit in the garden (17) except fruit from the tree of the knowledge of good and evil. If you eat of its fruit, you will surely die.*

Genesis 2:8-17 explained that God planted Adam in the center of garden (Genesis 2:9). The Lord God placed the man in the Garden of Eden to tend and to care for it (Genesis 2:15).

Genesis 2:(16) *But the Lord God gave him this warning: "You may freely eat any fruit in the garden (17) except fruit from the tree of the knowledge of good and evil. If you eat of its fruit, you will surely die." (18) And the Lord God said, "It is no good for the man to be alone. I will make a companion who will help him." (19) So the Lord God formed from the soil every kind of animal and bird. He brought them to Adam to see what he would call them, and Adam chose a name for each one. (20) He gave names to all the livestock, birds, and wild animals. But still there was no companion suitable for him.*

Adam's job description in Eden called for him to have dominion. Adam meditated and had conversations with God. He was the first prophet and king, and these assignments required work and responsibility. God gave instructions (Genesis 2:16) and wisdom to Adam about how to work and care for the Garden of Eden. It was Adam's job to care for all trees that produced delicious fruit (Genesis 2:9). Adam knew the whereabouts in the Garden of Eden and the center where the Tree of Life and Tree of the Knowledge of Good and Evil were located. Most of all, he remembered the instruction not to eat from the center tree, the Tree of the Knowledge of Good and Evil (Genesis 2:9). He learned to recognize the seasons to plant and harvest. Most of all, he learned to give thanks in offerings and tithes. The Tree of the Knowledge of Good and Evil and The Tree of Life were planted in the center of the garden. The Tree of Life is the Son of God, Jesus. Yes, Jesus was planted and spoken of in the beginning. God had a purpose for Adam and Jesus.

Adam was surrounded by treasures and rivers. There were four branches named the Pishon, Gihon, Tigris, and Euhrates. The lands were known as Havilah, Ethiopia, and Asshur. Treasures of gold, aromatic resin, and onyx stone were available on top of land. Adam gave a name to every living creature, even the serpent (Genesis 2:19-20). God walked and spoke to Adam in the Garden of Eden. Adam had dominion in the Garden and had no companion. Then *the Lord caused Adam to fall into a deep sleep. He took one of Adam's ribs and closed up the place from which he had taken it (Genesis 2:21). (22) Then the Lord made a woman from the rib and brought her to Adam.*

The Lord brought the woman to Adam and he had a revelation. In his words, *(23) "At last! "She is part of my own flesh and bone! She will be called 'woman' because she was taken from man."* God has a purpose for the unity of man and woman. (Genesis 2:24) *This explains why a man leaves his father and mother and is joined to his wife, and the two are united into one.* The serpent is introduced through a conversation with the woman in Genesis 3:1-5. However, Adam was with the woman and then ate the fruit (Genesis 3:6). After Adam ate, *their eyes were opened, and they suddenly felt shame at their nakedness.* (Genesis 3:7). *So they strung fig leaves together around their hips to cover themselves (8).* They used fig leaves to cover their nakedness.

When their judgment came, God was merciful and provided for Adam and Eve. After their judgment, *Adam named his wife Eve, because she would be the mother of all people everywhere (Genesis 3:20). (21) And the Lord God made clothing from animal skins for Adam and his wife.* The Lord showed Adam and Eve how to use cloth and animal skins to cover themselves. Adam still had dominion over the animals, but now he would have to hunt them for food, shelter, offerings, and clothing. Most of all, he would have to gather domestic animals daily for food resources and protect his family from some of these animals. Adam and Eve would have to work together to build a tent/shelter, garden, and farm. Also, God provided Adam and Eve with new information to eat from The Tree of Life. During the judgment, God said to the serpent:

"Because you have done this, you will be punished. You are singled out from all the domestic and wild animals of the whole earth

to be cursed. You will grovel on your belly (Genesis 3:14). *(15) From now on, you and the woman will be enemies and your offspring and her offspring will be enemies. He will crush your head, and you will strike his heel."*

(Genesis 3:22) *Then the Lord God said, "The people have become as we are, knowing everything, both good and evil. What if they eat the fruit of the tree of life? Then they will live forever!" (23) So the Lord God banished Adam and his wife from the Garden of Eden, and he sent Adam out to cultivate the ground from which he had been made. (24) After banishing them from the garden, the Lord God stationed mighty angelic beings to the East of Eden. And a flaming sword flashed back and forth, guarding to the tree of life.*

Let me encourage you that God is referring to Jesus as The Tree of Life. This indicates that Jesus was planted and manifested from the beginning to eternity. Jesus' victory over death was described when God described Jesus as the victor who will crush the serpent's head. Once again, Adam cultivated the land in a new place with his wife. Adam, the son of God (Luke 3:38d), took his experience as a priest (Genesis 2:16-17), prophet (Genesis 2:20), chief executive and empowerment officer (Genesis 2:15), husband (Genesis 2:23-24), king (Genesis 2:10-14) into this new place. It was hard, but he passed on his teachings to his sons Cain, Abel, and Seth. Adam lived 930 years and preached to Seth's generation about God, the Garden of Eden, and the Living Tree of Life until Noah. Adam's message to these generations was to have hope and prepare the next generations to build the Kingdom of God on earth as it is in Heaven. You have a responsibility to stand up and be a provider, teacher, messenger, manager, and champion in your unit known as your household. Like Adam, you have God's message to share and give to your generation and children's generation.

It is important for you to have a relationship with God to understand how to walk in dominion. Therefore, you need to grow and mature in the Jeremiah 29:11 plans for you through a relationship with God. It's important to establish a prayer life, learn how to pray, and understand the place, time, and seasons. This discipline is important for you to commit yourself to instruction and to hear the word of knowledge. Let me encourage you to step into your role as a champion. This means that you are a winner in every situation and can help others discover their Jeremiah 29:11 purposes. A champion shares their victory with others. Also, a champion is not threatened by others' Jeremiah 29:11 plans and purposes. Be a champion this season knowing that God has planted a Jeremiah 29:11 seed within you. Therefore, begin to view others with an end view in mind.

Still Point Moment: You have the victory to overcome anything! You have dominion! You are not alone or a victim in the plans God have for you. Take a moment to pray about your purpose and plans God has for you.

Still Transition Affirmations: *Commit everything you do to the Lord. Trust him, and he will help you* (Psalm 37:5). As you move forward on your Jeremiah 29:11 journey keep in mind these tips for success as they relate to still transition: be self-directed, resourceful, and proactive.

God's Plans for Man: Be Responsible

Now that you can look at your situation with an end view, you can walk in victory. In this section, "Responsibility," you will develop the mindset to be peaceful with yourself and others. This section is designed to empower you to be peaceful in every situation with yourself and people. Be patient with yourself and others in different walks of faith. Therefore, you have to be peaceful in your Jeremiah 29:11 assignment, people will challenge your faith and actions. Be encouraged as you read about responsibilities and commitments. These principles of peace are required as you work in your Jeremiah 29:11 assignments. The objective is to know that your faith has an assignment. As you continue to read, be still as you discover your Jeremiah 29:11 identities.

Still Point: *Choose a good reputation over riches, for being held in high esteem is better than having silver or gold (Proverbs 22:1). "People need more than bread for their life; they must feed on every word of God (Genesis 4:4)." (2) "Do not test the Lord your God (Genesis 4:7)." (3) "Get out of here, Satan, For the Scriptures say, You must worship the Lord your God; serve only him (Genesis 4:10)".*

Jesus, the High Priest, showed us how to resist the adversary's temptation. The scriptures stated that after Jesus resisted the Devil's temptation, *"Then the Devil went away, and angels came and cared for Jesus (Matthew 4:11).* We can look at this situation and say that Jesus had the victory because He knew and had faith in how the Word of God works. You have this same faith walking ability to resist the devil and avoid falling into traps by applying the word of God to the temptation. The Holy Spirit is present to comfort us when challenges arise in our seasons. You will know the Holy Spirit is present when you learn and recognize the fruits of the spirit which are *love, joy, peace, patience, kindness, goodness, faithfulness, gentleness, and self-control (Galatians 5:22).*

Let me encourage you to cultivate your Jeremiah 29:11 ground with seeds of the Spirit to reap a field to help you, your family, and others. Take claim of your responsibility to yourself, children, family, and your home. Get rid of excuses, blame, and "it's not my fault," because that is victim thinking. Victim thinking is a form of denial and an enemy to the plans God has for you. Victim thinking will keep you trapped in insecurity and fault finding. It can also keep your mind captive from the plans God has for you. Accept responsibility in your situation even if you feel hurt or angry.

Break the ground of denying responsibility and replace it with joy and happiness. These principles are keys in the plans God has for you. Cultivate the ground to the Jeremiah 29:11 plans with a renewed mind for the purposes. There is a devil on the prowl to steal your hope, seed, and harvest. The devil's plan has always been to kill, steal, and destroy the plans God has for you. The devil is a deceiver and thought he could stop God's plan for the human figure of the Tree of Life. In previous Old Testament generations, the devil tried different approaches to destroy and oppress the children of Israel. The devil's plan did not work. Jesus grew up in a town called Nazareth (Matthew 2:23). As Jesus grew, He went from Galilee to the Jordan River to be baptized by John (Matthew 3:13). The baptism had a purpose in Jesus and John's lives. The baptism symbolizes Jesus' obedience to His Heavenly Father. In addition to fulfilling John's purpose to baptize Jesus. This process led to his 40-day temptation and next level.

Then, Jesus was led out into the wilderness by the Holy Spirit to be tempted there by the Devil (Matthew 4:1). (2) For forty days and forty nights he ate nothing and became very hungry. (11) Then the Devil went away, and angels came and cared for Jesus.

(17) From then on, Jesus began to preach, "Turn from your sins and turn to God, because the Kingdom of Heaven is near."

Jesus' message to the people was to follow God's will and not his own (John 5:19); to do God's work (John 5:30); and speak God's word (John 5:30). This humble walk is part of your Jeremiah 29:11 plans and purpose. You have a responsibility to know the plans God has for you to trust and have hope. Therefore, you need to empty out hurt and baggage that are blocking your closeness to God. Make space in your heart right now by believing that Jesus as King of Kings and the living Tree of Life. You have a message to give to others. Be encouraged as you empty yourself to come close to know Jesus. As you read, you will see that when the disciples were called, they walked away from their familiar places. Their answer was conformation enough to leave everything and follow Jesus. Many crowds gathered around Jesus as He preached, fed the hungry, gave sight to the blind, and made the deaf hear. Jesus became close to the assembly of crowds because he deeply loved the people. In the scriptures, Jesus is portrayed as the one who empathized with the people.

He felt great pity for the crowds that came, because their problems were go great and they didn't know where to go for help. They were like sheep without a shepherd (Matthew9:36). (37) He said to his disciples, "This harvest is so great, but the workers are few. (38) So pray to the Lord who is in charge of the harvest; ask him to send out more workers for this field.

Jesus called his twelve disciples to him and gave them authority to cast out evil spirits and to heal every kind of disease and illness (Matthew 10:1). (2) Here are the names of the twelve apostles: Simon, also called Peter, Andrew, James (son of Zebedee), John, (3) Phillip, Bartholomew, Thomas, Matthew, James (son of Alphaeus), Thaddaeus,(4) Simon, and Judas Iscariot.

These twelve were *selected to be his regular companions, calling them apostles. He sent them out to preach, (Mark 3:15) and gave them authority to cast out demons.* Jesus sent these men out with instructions in Matthew 10:5-42. In the plans God has for you, it is important to sustain and protect your new life in Christ as a believer and follower. Salvation is yours in Jesus Christ. Make room in your heart to receive the plans and promises God has for you. When you come face-to-face with situations because of limitations, understand that Jesus is near with His hand out. Make the decision today to accept the Jeremiah 29:11 plans for you. God is going to use you to make changes in your family, community, and nation.

Step into your champion role with the responsibility to have faith in every situation. You will have to uphold a spiritual life with a prayer, mediation, and Bible reading time. This will help you to cultivate and know your Jeremiah 29:11 assignments. Be a champion this season following Jesus and understanding the plans God has for you.

Still Point Moment: Let me encourage you to let go and forgive yourself and others as you cultivate new knowledge and put your faith into action. Start helping others while you help yourself.

Still Transition Affirmations: *"This is the day which the Lord hath made. I will rejoice and be glad in it (Psalm 118: 24).* As you move forward on your Jeremiah 29:11 journey keep in mind these tips for success as they relate to still transition: be self-directed, resourceful, and proactive.

God's Plans for Man: Follow Jesus

You have the victory. The comfort of the Holy Spirit is available to guide, give counsel, and strengthen you. Comfort is written in the Jeremiah 29:11 plans for you. This section is written to encourage you that you're not alone in your assignment. You are not alone when you follow Jesus. The Holy Spirit, The Comforter, wants to lead you. Therefore, you have to make Jesus first in your Jeremiah 29:11 assignment, because your faith will get challenged. Be encouraged as you read this section "Follow Jesus." It takes the principle of trust to work in your Jeremiah 29:11 assignments. The objective is to know that your faith has an assignment to trust Jesus. As you continue to read, be still as you discover your Jeremiah 29:11 identities.

Still Point: *My heart is confident in you, O God; no wonder I can sing your praises! Wake up, my soul! (Psalm 108:1).*

Like the disciples, you will have teaching and testing moments as you continue to grow in the plans God has for you. The disciples traveled with Jesus to towns as He preached in the synagogues and expelled demons from people (Mark 1:39). These men were called regular companions (Mark 1:21 and 3:14). They traveled and ministered with Jesus from place to place. The news about Jesus quickly spread as people came from everywhere to witness the miracles. Crowds of people followed Jesus until they were convinced to believe. However, the Pharisees followed Jesus only to undermine his mission and new followers. Yet there were family members and people who tried to talk Jesus out of purpose.

Still, his hometown, Nazareth the people *who heard him were astonished. They asked. "Where did he get all his wisdom and the power to perform such miracles (Mark 6:2b)? (3) He's just the carpenter, the son of Mary and brother of James, Joseph, Judas, and Simon. And this sisters live right here among us." They were deeply offended and refused to believe in him.*

As you continue to cultivate the plans God has for you: pray, study, and surround yourself with acquaintances on the similar Jeremiah 29:11 mission seeking. You may experience rejection and closed ears from the people who know you. Also, people that are close to you may try to undermine your purposes and achievements. Understand that Jesus was rejected from the people of his hometown. Be encouraged that Jesus said, *"Anyone who does God's will is my brother and sister and mother (Mark 3:35)/"(Luke 8:21).* The disciples grew into their Kingdom building assignments as apostles. God had a plan for them to prepare the people for Pentecost (Act 2).

God had plans for Peter according to Act 2:14-17. Peter addressed the crowd out of his relationship with God. God's hands were on Peter as he addressed the crowd at nine o'clock in the morning. Peter made public to new and old believers about Joel 2:28-29 prophecy of the next generation's sons and daughters spiritual gifts. This is because God's Word remains the same forever. Also, Peter revealed Jesus as Lords and Messiah. Peter's message to the crowd included to repenting, being baptized in the name of Jesus, asking for forgiveness of their sins, and receiving the Holy Spirit.

God used Peter in a mighty way. First, Peter helped and healed a lame beggar. In his approach, he helped the man get up and stand at a gate called Beautiful. By faith, the man became strong and stood up. Let me encourage you to pray in the name of Jesus and stand up in your situation. Second, the gate called Beautiful had a plan and purpose for spectators to believe in the name of Jesus plans for a miracle. The name of Jesus will sustain, cover, and encourage you at your new gate. The name of Jesus will change your situation because of power in His name. Therefore, let me encourage you to change your mind-set into the Beautiful-Gate which is your divine self. There is a Beautiful-Gate in your Jeremiah 29:11 plan and path. This gate is your immediate change and transformation manifested into the plans God has for you. Hold on while you are in this shift to your next level.

You are on your way to mature and be a champion in the Lord. The process to discovering the plans that are designed for you includes a divine transformation. Your testimony to others is your daily walk with Jesus and other believers. The name of Jesus will bring immediate change to the labels people put on your life just as it did for the man in the story. Peter spoke the Word, the preordained Word spoken in this man's life. This man appeared with Peter in court, and became a witness of the Power of the name of Jesus. Let me encourage you that you are wonderfully made according to Psalm 139:9. People are going to see your life turn around. Your turnaround is the message you will share with others so they will believe in the name of Jesus.

Still Point Moment: Get ready to work in the plans God has for you. You need to have faith in God to understand your purpose. Good success is written in the Jeremiah 29:11 plans for you. Therefore, you do not have to worry or try to impress anybody.

Still Point Transition: *Jeremiah 29:12 Then you will call on me and come and pray to me, and I will listen to you. (13) You will seek me and find me when you seek me with all your heart.* Call and pray to the Lord! You will find the Lord, when you seek Him. Be encouraged this season. As you move forward on your Jeremiah 29:11 journey keep in mind these tips for success as they relate to transition: be self-directed, resourceful, and proactive.

God's Plans for Man: Love

Jesus had moments when He was alone and to pray in the wilderness (Mark 1:35; Luke 4:42). You are not alone in the plans God has for you. Pray, study the Bible, and make space in your heart for the plans God has for you. Jesus demonstrated his love as He was falsely accused by the Pharisees, denied by Peter, and sentenced to death.

Then a mighty roar rose from the crowd, and with one voice they shouted, "Kill him, and release Barabbas to us (Luke 23:18)!" (Barabbas was in prison for murder and for taking part in an insurrection in Jerusalem against the government.) (20) Pilate argued with them, because he wanted to release Jesus. (21) But they shouted, "Crucify him! Crucify him!" (22) For the third time he demanded, "Why? What crime has he committed? I found no reason to sentence him to death. I will therefore flog him and let him go." (23) But the crowd shouted louder and louder for Jesus' death, and their voices prevailed. (24) So, Pilate sentenced Jesus to die as they demanded. (25) As they had requested, he released Barabbas, the man in prison for insurrection and murder. But he delivered Jesus over to them to do as they wished.

Jesus demonstrated real love (I John 3:16) by taking Barabbas' place. You are like Barabbas. Remember that Jesus took your place on the cross. You were given mercy and second chances to get life right with God. Jesus took the place of Barabbas, a prisoner, and received a death sentence. Pilate, the ruler at the time, wanted to release Jesus because of his innocence. However, Pilate listened to the crowd and released Barabbas. Pilate's lack of leadership made Jesus a prisoner, beaten, and sentenced to be put to death.

As they led Jesus away, Simon of Cyrene, who was coming in from the country just then was forced to follow Jesus and carry his cross (Luke 23:26). I can imagine Jesus' body being too weak to carry the cross. However, by chance, Simon was in the crowd and was picked to carry Jesus' cross. The scriptures do not give detail about why Simon was chosen, but he was strong enough to carry Jesus' cross. I believe Simon was an answered prayer for Jesus. Simon's purpose was to show us that God will still provide help when our companions deny and abandon us. Like Simon, we are servants of the Living Tree of Life. Jesus is the Living Tree of Life as it was written in the beginning. The cross that Jesus was to be nailed to was carried by Simon of Cyrene. The cross had a purpose to end the curse and fulfill Christ prophecy. Its purpose was to be planted in the land of Skull. Simon purpose was to be a temporary helper and supporter during Jesus' most critical need.

According to the scriptures, the cross was laid on the ground once it reached the top. Jesus lay on top of the cross. The soldiers nailed Jesus' hands and feet to the cross. Then, the cross was lifted by the soldiers, with Jesus nailed to it. Lastly, the cross was planted in the ground fulfilling prophesy. This prophesy was fulfilled and spoken by the Old Testament prophets that Jesus, the Living Tree of Life, was planted as the sacrificial lamb. Jesus, took our sins to the cross at noon. Then darkness fell across the whole land until three o'clock (Luke 23:44). His obedience symbolized love.

Jesus hung between two men who were given criminal sentences. *Two others, both criminals, were led out to be executed with him (Luke 23:32). (33) Finally, they came to a place called the Skull. All three were crucified there-Jesus on the center cross, and the two criminals on either side.* Jesus had a purpose to be planted in the middle of two men sentenced to be crucified. Both criminals were witnesses to Jesus' miracles and teachings. However, only one of them perceived that Jesus was innocent. In addition, this nameless man received the Kingdom at the very moment of the threat of death. Jesus witnessed to one of the criminals, then prayed and asked the Heavenly Father to forgive others while on the cross.

God's purpose and plans for you happened at the cross where Jesus was hung. In the Garden of Eden, the Tree of Life was planted in the center. Also, Jesus' cross was planted in the center at the place called Skull. Jesus, The Living Tree, was crucified in a dried place called Skull. The Living Tree of Life was nailed on the cross, and planted in the ground as a sacrifice so we could have everlasting life. Therefore, *the curse on the ground (Genesis 3:17)* and *the struggle to scratch a living from it (Genesis 3:18)* was broken. This curse and struggle was broken as Jesus hung on the cross.

The burial of Jesus' body was the next purpose to cover and heal the ground where Abel's blood cried out to God (Genesis 4:10). Jesus' body had to be placed in the tomb. The tomb had a purpose for Jesus' body. Joseph, a good and righteous man and a member of the Jewish high council had been waiting for the Kingdom of God to come. God had a plan for Joseph to become Jesus' undertaker.

He went to Pilate and asked for Jesus' body (Luke 23:52). (53) Then he took the body down from the cross and wrapped it in a long linen cloth and laid it in a new tomb that had been carved out of rock. (54) This as done late on Friday afternoon, the day of preparation for the Sabbath.

Joseph had faith and waited for the Kingdom of God to come. Let me encourage you to have faith in the Kingdom of God. Most of all, have courage to carry out your faith duties like Joseph. It was Jewish custom to rest on the Sabbath. Therefore, Joseph's duties honored God's plans. Our bodies are returned to the ground, from dust, and to the dust we will return (Genesis 3:19b). God had a plan for Joseph to claim and care for Jesus' body, that Friday evening. Jesus' body was now wrapped and placed in a tomb in preparation for the Sabbath. Jesus' body rested in a tomb on the Sabbath Day! Jesus rose from the tomb on Sunday morning! Love is the ultimate example to commit, be responsible, and finish God's plan.

There is victory in the plans God has for you and your family. Let me encourage you to rise up to be the champion God called you to be through a Jeremiah 29:11 identity. Increase your work, responsibility, and values by helping someone else. You are designed to be a blessing to others. In this process you need to ask God about your process. Some things in your life need to die in the process so that new things can be born in your Jeremiah 29:11 assignments. The love of Jesus saved you from sin and eternal death when you accepted Salvation. Envision the plans God has for you to coming to pass while you experience transitions. Therefore, you have to trust God when you don't understand or see the plans.

You are not alone as you continue to cultivate the ground in the plans God has for you. There is a message about God that you have to share with the people near you. Like Jesus, the Living Tree of Life, you need to be God-centered. Make time and develop a relationship with God through prayer and time alone. God-centeredness is important as you continue to cultivate the ground.

Still Point Moment: Be encouraged from this day forward and know that God has plans for you! Next, you need to share your message about God with others, so they can live and discover the Kingdom of God. The people you witness to have a message to share with others. Therefore, break the ground in the plans God has for you and share the message about the Living Tree of Life and the victory that happened at the cross.

Still Transition Affirmations: *God is our refuge and strength, always ready to help in times trouble (Psalm 46:1).* As you move forward on your Jeremiah 29:11 journey keep in mind these tips for success as they relate to transition: be self-directed, resourceful, and proactive.

Section One Reflection:
Discover Your Jeremiah 29:11 Purpose

You have a Jeremiah 29:11 purpose. Commit to your Jeremiah 29:11 assignments. God's plan and purpose for men to have dominion in the positions as sons, husbands, brothers, cousins, uncles, and friends. Most of all, His plan is for them to be position according to Ephesians 4:11 as apostles, prophets, evangelists, pastors and teachers. Be responsible and follow Jesus. Be God-centered in your Jeremiah 29:11 identity and assignment.

In this process be patient and view your situation with an end view. Anchor your faith daily in Jeremiah 29:11. Be encouraged and know that God is not finished with you yet. This means that your circumstances do not determine where you are going. Let me encourage you to continue to walk in their Jeremiah 29:11 plans with hope and believe that you belong to God. Discover your Jeremiah 29:11 purposes by committing to your assignment, being responsible, following Jesus, and loving yourself and others. Be motivated as you to go to your next level. Somebody is watching you and learning from you how to live in his Jeremiah 29:11 identities.

Section Two:
Have Integrity

God's Plans for Man: Know Your Purpose

You may have to pause or be still to understand your purpose. You can look at your situation with an end view; however, you need a strategy. You need a strategy to connect with your purpose. This section is written for you to pause and be still to connect to your assignment. Be encouraged as you read this section, "Your Purpose." At times, you may have to pause and be still for principles to work accordingly in your Jeremiah 29:11 assignments. The objective is to know that your faith has an assignment. As you continue to read, be still as you discover your Jeremiah 29:11 identities.

Still Point: *Praise the Lord! I will thank the Lord with all my heart as I meet with godly people (Psalm 111:1). (2) How amazing are the deeds of the Lord! All who delight in him should ponder them.*

Schedule A Meeting With God

(Genesis 6:5) Now the Lord observed the extent of the people's wickedness, and he saw that all their thoughts were consistently and totally evil. (6) So the Lord was sorry He had ever made them. It broke his heart. (8) But Noah found favor with the Lord. (9) This is the history of Noah and his family. Noah was a righteous man, the only blameless man living on earth at the time. He consistently followed God's Will and enjoyed a close relationship with Him.

You may be the first person to leave home, move to another place, branch into your own business, or complete a degree. You can complete your goals with a plan and principles of faith and responsibilities. You have a responsibility to work and show up on time to your assignment. Noah was a preacher, and God gave him a new assignment which included something that was a first. Noah was the first preacher to build an ark and preach about the rain that was about to come. The plans God has for your purpose includes a crowd. You may look foolish to people, but not to God. While Noah worked, the people watched, gossiped, and spectated. This crowd was used to hearing Noah's preaching about God, not building a structure. Noah and his family worked, preached, and built the Ark. The Ark had a purpose to save, provide shelter, and be a place of refuge for the next plan of God. You need a relationship with God to know your Jeremiah 29:11 purposes and plans for you and your family. It's important for you and your family members to work collectively in your Jeremiah 29:11 plans. You may need to have a patient temperament to work with people, especially family. Therefore, it is important to be aware of the things that push your buttons. Those are the things you need to change as you work with God's people. Keep in mind that you are training and working with others to become champions in their future Jeremiah 29:11 assignments. Don't miss your opportunity to be a teacher in the experience and assignment with your family.

Now let's examine the facts about Noah. *2 Peter 2:(5a) And God did not spare the ancient world-except for Noah and his family of seven. Noah warned the world of God's righteous judgment.* The crowd watched Noah and his family build the ark. They stopped and asked questions about the ark but they did not understand rain (anointing), flood (covering), nor the Ark (God's dwelling) for God's future purposes. Therefore, you are designed to be a gift and life-saver to others.

Genesis (6:13) So God said to Noah, "I have decided to destroy all living creatures, for the earth is filled with violence because of them. Yes, I will wipe them all from the face of the earth! (14) Make a boat from resinous wood and seal it with tar, inside and out. Then construct decks and stalls throughout its interior. (15) Made it 450 feet wide, and 45 feet high. (16) Construct an opening all the way around the boat, 18 inches below the roof. Then put three decks inside the boat-bottom, middle, and upper-and put a door in the side. (17) Look! I am about to cover the earth with a flood that will destroy every living thing. Everything on earth will die! (18) But I solemnly swear to keep you safe in the boat, with your wife and your sons and their wives.

The people did not understand what they saw. These wicked people were the generations of Cain and were described as evil and wicked. *(Hebrews 11:7) It was by faith that Noah built an ark to save his family from the flood. He obeyed God, who warned him about something that had never happened before. By his faith he condemned the rest of the world and was made right in God's sight.* Because Noah consistently followed God's Will and enjoyed a close relationship with Him, God gave him favor and his family was saved! *2 Peter 2:(5b) Then God destroyed the whole world of ungodly people with a vast flood.* Noah enjoyed his relationship with God. Also, Noah was meeting God in secret through prayer about how to build the ark. Then the day came when the Lord said to Noah,
"Go into the boat with all your family, for among all the people of the earth, I consider you alone to be righteous (Genesis 7:1). (2) Take along seven pairs of each animal that I have approved for eating and for sacrifice, and take one pair of each of the others."

Let me encourage you to position yourself to hear God say, "GO!" and "TAKE!" You must to have a relationship to be able to recognize His Voice and obey His Command. According to Ecclesiastes, there are going to be seasons in your life when you need to have a listening ear and spirit to receive God's message. Like Noah, you have to remain in God's will to receive instructions about moving to the next destination of your life. You must complete your assignments to go to the next destination God wants to take you. Let's take a close look at some scriptures where Noah received instructions from God.

Genesis 7:5 So Noah did exactly as the Lord had commanded him. (6) He was 600 years old when the flood came, (7) and he went aboard the boat to escape-he and his wife and his sons and their wives. (8) With them were all the various kinds of animals-those approved for eating and sacrifice and those that were not-along with all the birds and other small animals.

Noah and his family were in a safe place while God was at work. God is revealed as shelter, refuge, an Ark, and protector. Noah's obedience to be the first and trust God saved his family during the flood season. As you press forward and closer to your purpose, seek God and build up your faith. Follow God while on the path and listen for His voice. Believe that God schedules meetings with us in our Jeremiah 29:11 plans.

Another example of scheduled meetings took place between God and Abraham, who was the father of the covenant and promise. Abraham had several meetings with God. In one meeting, *Genesis 22:1, "God tested Abraham's faith and obedience, Abraham!" God called. "Yes," he replied. "Here I am." (2) Take your son, your only son- yes Isaac, whom you love so much-and go to the land of Moriah. Sacrifice him there as a burnt offering on one of the mountains, which I will point out to you."*

God gave Abraham a difficult assignment; however, he believed that, *"God will provide (Genesis 22:8)."* Abraham believed and obeyed. Then, (Genesis 22:13) God provided a ram caught by its horns in a bush. The ram became the sacrifice. It's through your test and trials that God is revealed. God is revealed as a provider to Abraham and Isaac's test. Also, God gave Noah strength to build an ark and provided shelter from the flood. No matter your situation, God will provide you with endurance to complete your Jeremiah 29:11 plans for your future. My brother, build your faith by having a relationship with God. As Noah believed in God's plans to build an ark, his family was saved and received favor and access inside the ark. Your faith in God's plans will save you and your family. Your faith may be condemned by a crowd, but you will be made right in God's sight. Make time for God.

Let me encourage you to schedule a meeting with God. God will continue to show up in the Jeremiah 29:11 plans of his chosen people. Believe that you are chosen to be a worker in the Kingdom of God. Make time with God to connect and understand your Jeremiah 29:11 plans. Be a champion and schedule a meeting with God so that you will know the Jeremiah 29:11 plans for you and your family. Get ready to receive your Jeremiah 29:11 assignments. Also, get ready to be the first, have new ideas, and reach your new level by scheduling a meeting with God. No matter what your situation looks like, you are in a safe place. God is working with you to become a champion for the Kingdom.

Still Point Moment: What does your meeting with God look like? Are you on time? Are you ready to do something different than others? Noah and Abraham had a relationship with God, and committed to their assignments. Please understand that the plan and purpose designed for your life is to enhance Heaven on Earth for generations of tomorrow. Schedule a meeting with God through daily prayer, devotion, and worship to get closer to His Glory. Meetings with God will help you recognize His voice and understand your assignment. The scriptures in Genesis 6:13-18 show you that God had a meeting with Noah about how to build the exterior and interior of the ark. God showed Noah in Genesis 6:17 the revelation of the flood and its purpose. *So Noah did everything exactly as God had commanded him (Genesis 6:22).* Therefore, know your purpose in the plans God has for you by scheduling a meeting with God.

Still Transitions Affirmation: *You will keep on guiding me with your council (Psalm 73: 24).* As you move forward on your Jeremiah 29:11 journey keep in mind these tips for success as they relate to still transition: be self-directed, resourceful, and proactive.

God's Plans for Man: Know and Recognize Your Season

Every day is an opportunity to spend time with our Heavenly Creator and in the word. The purpose of this section, "Know and Recognize Your Season," is to understand what God has said to you. Let me encourage you to align your plans with the promises God has for you. This is your season to get out of unproductive relationships with people, places, and things. Be encouraged as you read this section on the principle of "cut off." This season, you will cut people, places, and things off to work in your Jeremiah 29:11 assignments. The objective is to know that your faith has an assignment. As you continue to read, be still as you discover your Jeremiah 29:11 identities.

Still Point: *Give your burdens to the Lord, and he will take care of you. He will not permit the godly to slip and fall (Psalm 55:22).*

It's Time to Know and Recognize Your Season

It's time to see your season and prepare for your purpose. King Solomon was blessed in many ways; however, he intermarried with hundreds of wives who worshiped false idols. His castle was filled with different spirits which lead him to worship these idols and, in turn, lose his kingdom and integrity with God and his people. Solomon lost sight of God. It's time for you, man of God, to clean out the house. It's time for you to make room for your blessing. It's time for you to let go of those things and people distracting you from your blessing.

It's time to find your purpose because your children's future is depending on you to be responsible, to work, and to commit to the Jeremiah 29:11 plans. God wants to bless you; therefore you need to have a relationship with Him! What are you asking God? King Solomon asked God for, *"an understanding mind to govern His people and know the difference between right and wrong" (I Kings 3:9).*

God was pleased with Solomon's reply and blessed him with an understanding mind such as no one else had/will ever have (I

Kings 3:12). God told him that He was going to bless him with riches and honor because Solomon did not ask for it (I King 3:13). As you begin this season, position yourself to receive your blessing. *Psalm 1:2 But they delight in doing everything the Lord wants; day and night they think about his law. (3) They are like trees planted along the riverbank, bearing fruit each season without fail. Their leaves never wither, and in all they do, they prosper.* Get planted, so you won't miss another season. Get planted to bear the fruit of love, peace, joy, and understanding. Remember your gifts are designed to bless others. This means to seek God in prayer more! In Ecclesiastes 3:1-8, Solomon explains seasons and time with respect to blessings.

(1) There is a time for everything, a season for every activity under heaven. (2) A time to be born and a time to die. A time to plant and a time to harvest. (3) A time to kill and a time to heal. A time to tear down and a time to rebuild. (4) A time to cry and a time to laugh. A time to grieve and a time to dance. (5) A time to scatter stones and a time to gather stones. A time to embrace and a time to turn away. (6) A time to search and a time to lose. A time to keep and a time to throw away. (7) A time to tear and a time to mend. A time to be quiet and a time to speak up. (8) A time to love and a time to hate. A time for war and a time for peace.

Get to know and access your season by aligning it to the plans God has for you. Ask and pray to God for wisdom and understanding to operate in your Jeremiah 29:11 identity. Solomon explained it is important to be wise in your seasons and recognize changes, you need to trust God as He continues to add and subtract in order to make the way for you to fulfill your purpose. Let me encourage you to be a champion when it's time to let go of things, places, and people that are holding you back! Get yourself and house-unit in order by listening to God and not to the crowd. Remember, seasons change, you change, but God never changes. Have integrity as God continues to promote you. Be on time to your appointment with God through prayer, mediation, and Bible study. Most of all, be patient as you transition by holding on to your faith and vision of your Jeremiah 29:11 plans and purpose. Be a champion and recognize your season and set the necessary goals and manage your time to walk in your Jeremiah 29:11 assignments.

Still Point Moment: Get your heart and house in order in the plans God has for you. Like Solomon, you have to make room for spiritual growth. Let me encourage you to make time for God in prayer and humbly manage your gifts. Make the changes you need to recognize your season; and then align and adjust as needed to be committed to your assignment.

Still Transition Affirmations: *For, I can do everything with the help of Christ who gives me the strength I need (Philippians 4:13).* As you move forward on your Jeremiah 29:11 journey keep in mind these tips for success as they relate to transition: be self-directed, resourceful, and proactive.

God's Plans for Man: Be Teachable

Get ready to learn in the plans God has for you. The type of learning spirit you need is a thirsty spirit. You need a teachable spirit because your faith will get challenged in the Jeremiah 29:11 plans for you. This section is written to encourage you to have a teachable spirit in your assignment. Be encouraged as you read this section about being teachable. This is a major principle in your Jeremiah 29:11 assignments. The objective is to know that your faith has an assignment. As you continue to read, be still as you discover your Jeremiah 29:11 identities.

Still Point: *Psalm 42:1 As the deer pants for streams of water, so I long for you, O God. (2) I thirst for God, the living God. When can I come and stand before him?*

Be Like the Deer

Imagine that you are going to the theatre to watch a play. In this play, there are only three characters: the deer, a tree, and water. How would an individual play the roles of these abstracts, yet they are all created by God? I can imagine the deer, tree, and water defending their purposes or value. Yet, even though the tree, water, and deer are different they each have a purpose to serve each other. Can the deer have a bad day? Yes, the deer can have a bad day. Deers travel and live in herds led by a leader. The deer has predators and enemies seeking to hunt and kill him. A family of deers can get separated when getting chased or hiding by a predator. Have you ever been separated from your family? Deer families separate for safety and life issues. Can a deer get discouraged? Yes, the deer can get discouraged and tired from running and hiding. Life can make us tired. Let me encourage you to operate in hope even when you are tired. *Psalm 42:5 Why am I discouraged? Why so sad? I will put my hope in God! I will praise him again- my Savior and (6) my God!*

Psalm 1:3 They are like trees planted along the riverbank, bearing fruit each season without fail. The leaves never wither, and in all they do, they prosper." Be like the tree-planted near the water, stand tall, and become a blessing. Be like the tree that bears good fruit and be ready to bless somebody in your field. Your fruit is designed to be a blessing to others.

Here's a summary of the play. The deer is you, thirsty for the taste of the Lord. God's favor has flavor and only His fountain can fill our empty wells. The tree is you, standing tall and bearing fruit to share with other deer in your path. You have a choice to bless people with your fruit and lead them to the fountain of life; or curse them. As you know, deer frighten easily just like people who feel threatened or were misguided, abused, and misused. Fruit actions lead people to the source of the fruit you bear. When you stand tall like the tree, you make yourself the "fruit-bearer." As the fruit-bearer, you'll never know the deer that God is going to place in your path. So be ready to share your fruit and give the deer time to make its way to the water.

In the conclusion of the play, the tree encourages us to stay close and to stay connected to the vine, and to be planted near the fountain of life. What is the vine? Jesus is the vine and you are the branches (John 15:5a). *Those who remain in me, and I in them, will produce much fruit. For apart from me you can do nothing (John 15:5b).* Abide in God and reap your abundance. Share your fruit and abundance with others and pray for the deer in your path. A deer will come across your path because of your fruit and your heavenly fountain source. Also, deer will come in your path thirsty so let the fruits of the spirit guide them to the everlasting fountain.

The deer and tree understood their purposes: to value and love each other and abide close to the vine's resources. Why? Because, *The earth is the Lord's, and the fullness thereof; the world, and they that dwell therein.* Be a rescuer and help any deer(s) that come in your path to escape traps of life. Share your fruit from the vine's resource to help someone recover. Your assignment is to stand tall like the tree and be ready to be used by God. As you stay committed to your purpose make space in your heart to remember that God wants you to, *"stay jointed to me and my words remain in you, you may ask any request you like, and it will be granted (John 15:7)!"*

You are stronger in the plans God has for you because of what you have been through and overcame. Let me encourage you to hold on while God is shifting your situation to get you prepared for your next level. The Jeremiah 29:11 seed is deeply rooted when you get connected. Right now everything you've experienced has been part of the Jeremiah 29:11 plans for you. Every place you've lived, worked, worshiped God, and schools attended or graduated from were part of your training ground. Reflect on the time you spent sowing seeds in those fields. The people you've encountered or had relationships with were metaphorical doors. This means that people can open or close their resources to your purpose with help, shelter, clothing, advice, or opportunity.

Some people are in your life for a season as doors to help you successfully reach your harvest. Your harvest should be resources that look like owed property, a diploma, degree, employment, friendships, family, and partnership/organizations. Others are in your life for a season as doors to take you to and from your harvest. These individuals constantly withdraw from your harvest and never return a thank you, pay you back, and come up with excuses why they won't return or add back what they borrowed from your harvest. Let me encourage you to close the door on the people constantly withdrawing from your life. The consequences of not closing doors to these people will become a revolving door. Revolving doors are a bad cycle in your life. Be a champion and close and lock the revolving doors which include people, places, and things. Be encouraged as you cultivate your ground in the plans God has for you. Your self-image and culture will change as God adds to your life and new seasons.

Still Point Moment: Do you see the life lessons in this play? You have a role to encourage others with your fruit like the tree and not interrupt their worship at the fountain. The tree did not disturb the deer in its worship at the fountain. The tree watched and prayed for the deer. There may be people in your path that God has assigned for you to pray and watch over or even bless. When you abide in the vine, you become friends with Jesus.

You are my friends if you obey me (John 15:14). (15) I no longer call you servants, because a master doesn't confide in his servants. Now you are my friends, since I have told you everything the Father has told me. (16) You didn't choose me. I chose you. I appointed you to go and produce fruit that will last, so that the Father will give you whatever you ask for, using my name. (17) I command you to love each other.

Still Transition Affirmations: *But those that wait on the Lord will find strength. They will fly high on wings like eagles. They will run and not grow weary. They shall walk and not faint. (Isaiah 40:31).* As you move forward on your Jeremiah 29:11 journey keep in mind these tips for success as they relate to transition: be self-directed, resourceful, and proactive.

Section Two Reflection:
Have Integrity

Have integrity to make the right choices when you think people are not looking. Integrity, responsibility, and commitment are required in your Jeremiah 29:11 assignments.

Trust God even if you do not see or understand the plans and purpose. At times, you may have to pause and be still while principles to have faith, work, be responsible, and commitment work for you in your Jeremiah 29:11 assignments. You have the ability to walk by faith, power, authority, and by the Holy Spirit. Your faith has an assignment; therefore you need to have a meeting with God.

Be still as you discover your Jeremiah 29:11 identity. Ask and pray to God for wisdom and understanding to operate in you Jeremiah 29:11 identities. Let me encourage you to position yourself to have a relationship to be able to recognize His Voice and obey His Command. You can develop your relationship with God through prayer, meditation, reading the Bible, and becoming a member of church. Start paying attention to your environments by getting to know the people with no strings attached. Also, help make improvements to the people, places, and things you have access. As you get blessed, share your blessings, fruit, and abundance with others. Most of all, pray for the deer(s) in your path. Your integrity is being watched by others. Therefore, show up to your meetings with God to understand and receive wisdom to help and work in your accessed places. This relationship is important to understand the Jeremiah 29:11 plans God has for you. There are things you have not seen or experienced supernaturally that God is getting you ready for according to His purpose.

Section Three:
Have Faith

God's Plan for Man: Believe

Still Point: *The law of the Lord is perfect, reviving the soul. The decrees of the Lord are trustworthy, making wise the simple (Psalm 19:7). (8) The commandments of the Lord are right, bringing joy to the heart. The commands of the Lord are clear, giving insight to life. (9a) Reverence or the Lord is pure, lasting forever.*

You need to study and meditate on the Word of God as you go through. The Word of God kept in your heart will be like a bridge to connect you to your purpose. This section is written for you to believe God in your assignment. Be encouraged as you read this section, "Believe." It takes this principle to work in your Jeremiah 29:11 assignments. The objective is to know that your faith has an assignment and do not be afraid to walk in the Jeremiah 29:11 plans and purpose for you. As you continue to read, be still as you discover your Jeremiah 29:11 identities.

Gabriel's Good News to Zechariah!

Luke 1:5 It all begins with a Jewish priest, Zechariah, who lived when Herod was king of Judea. Zechariah was a member of priestly order Abijah. His wife, Elizabeth, was also from the priestly line of Aaron. (6) Zechariah and Elizabeth were righteous in God's eyes, careful to obey all the Lord's commandments and regulations. (7) They had no children because Elizabeth was barren, and now they were both very old. (8) One day Zechariah was serving God in the Temple, for his order was on duty that week. (9) As was the custom for the priest, he was chosen by lot to enter the sanctuary and burn incense in the Lord's presence. (10) While the incense was being burned, a great crowd stood outside praying. (11) Zechariah was in the sanctuary when an angel of the Lord appeared, standing to the right of the incense after. (12) Zechariah was overwhelmed with fear. (13) But the angel said, "Don't be afraid, Zechariah! For God has heard your prayer, and your wife, Elizabeth, will bear you a son! And you are to name him John. (14) You will have great joy and gladness, and many will rejoice with you at his birth, (15) for he will be great in the eyes of the Lord. He must never touch wine or liquor, and he will be filled with Holy Spirit, even before his birth. (16) And he will persuade man Israelites to turn to the Lord their God. (17) He will be a man with the spirit and power of Elijah, the prophet of old. He will precede the coming of the Lord, preparing the people for his arrival. He will turn the hearts of the fathers to their children, and he will change disobedient minds to accept godly wisdom." (18) Zechariah said to the angel, "How can I know this will happen? I'm an old man now, and my wife is also along in years."(19) Then the angel said, "I am Gabriel! I stand in the very presence of God. It was he who sent me to bring you this good news! (20) And now, since you didn't believe what I said, you won't be able to speak until the child is born. For my words will certainly come true at the proper time." (21) Meanwhile, the people were waiting for Zechariah to come out, wondering why he was taking so long. (22) When finally did come out, he couldn't speak to them. Then they realized from his gestures that he must have seen a vision in the Temple sanctuary. (23) He stayed at the Temple until his tem of service was over, and then he returned home. (24) Soon afterward his wife, Elizabeth, became pregnant and went into seclusion for five months. (25) "How kind the Lord is!" she exclaimed. "He has taken away my disgrace of having no children!"

Lessons to Take From Zechariah

Lesson 1: Zechariah was on duty in the Temple and serving God when he *became overwhelmed with fear (Luke 1:8)-(12)*. You can develop a comforting spirit when you keep a regular routine. Zechariah had given up on expecting God to produce previous prayers. Your prayers are seeds planted in the Heaven's realm. Also, your prayers are already manifested when you have faith. Therefore, when you pray, believe that it's already done! Let me encourage you not to give up expecting God to produce a harvest. God is increasing your territory because He is in control of your field. In this season, you need to keep your faith on duty. At times, a person can get caught in the web of routine and their faith gets caught familiar. The weight of burdens and secret doubts can surface when external conditions are barren. You may ask, "How am I supposed to respond to God when my faith is in a web?" The answer is to keep your faith by believing God for miracles, signs, and wonders. When your results appear barren or in the dark, *"Jesus said, 'I am the light of the world. If you follow me you won't be stumbling through the darkness, because you will have the light that leads to life (John 8:12)."* Take back your thinking, and get it out the web. Wait on God with expectation. He is working in your Jeremiah 29:11 plans and purpose. Therefore, you cannot get comfortable where you are at because God is not finished with you.

Lesson 2: *A great crowd stood outside praying (Luke 1:10-12)* when an angel of the Lord appeared, standing to the right of the incense alter. *(Luke 1:12) Zechariah was overwhelmed with fear.* It's time to examine your internal operation. Are you operating in: Fear or Faith? Fear will paralyze your faith walk. Fear will keep you barren and in the dark. Zechariah responded in fear and doubt to Gabriel's message. Zechariah's doubt was entangled with unbelief because he stopped expecting a child. The lesson you can learn from Zechariah's response is to respond to good news with faith.

Zechariah came to the temple in his regular routine, but he wasn't expecting his prayers to get answered. He accepted Elizabeth's label as barren because they never had any children. Be cautious about a regular routine or label. You have to be ready to "Go!" when God says "Go!" Today, begin to operate in great expectation that God will answer and supply all your needs. Therefore, you need to overcome anxiety (Philippians 4:13) with the Word of God. Be encouraged, and do not give yourself a label or allow doubt to creep in your thoughts. Be encouraged and know that God is not finished with you. Therefore, don't accept the labels people may give you because you have a Jeremiah 29:11 outcome with hope and prosperity.

Lesson 3: While Gabriel delivered the good message to Zechariah, the crowd was outside the temple praying. In worship, the presence of God is welcomed. It was tradition for the priest to; *enter the sanctuary and burn incense in the Lord's presence (Luke 1:9).* Therefore, when you worship, expect the presence of God to come while you worship alone, in a gathering, and even if there is a great crowd standing outside praying (Luke 1:10). Expect God to take you to the next levels of your life and speak to your prayer petitions. Have hope in God through a relationship. You need to have a prayer life with God. A prayer life includes talking and praying to God about situations and for others. God hears your prayer petitions. Your faith actions include trusting and believing in the plans God has for you.

Lesson 4: God hears your prayer petitions! *Luke 1:(13-15) for he will be great in the eyes of the Lord.* The Angel had the answer while Zechariah operated in unbelief. Unbelief is the action of operating in fear and it can abort or terminate the blessings and new levels that comes with an assignment. Fear will keep you in the dark and cause you to respond to God's plan in doubt. Gabriel is delivering Zechariah's answered prayer and he responds, *"How can I know this will happen? I'm an old man now, and my wife is also along in years (Luke 1:18)."* You have to be ready to receive. You cannot receive your answer when you are operating in denial and unbelief. This mind-set will block your understanding and receiving from God. God wants you to stay in touch with Him though worship, prayer, and fasting. You don't know how or when your blessing is going to appear. Therefore, you have to believe that your answer is going to come. Unbelief will rob of your praise to receive and rejoice to good news. Therefore, begin to praise God for your blessing to come through. Walk out of your barren thinking and into the "light" of faith. Receive the plans God has for you.

Lesson 5: God will test your faith. Discouragement builds up stress and unforgiveness. When God gave Gabriel the message to deliver to Zechariah, the angel already knew his response. *(19) Then the angel said, "I am Gabriel! I stand in the very presence of God. It was he who sent me to bring you this good news! (20) And now, since you didn't believe what I said, you won't be able to speak until the child is born. For my words will certainly come true at the proper time."* Gabriel shut Zechariah's mouth before speaking against his Jeremiah 29:11 purpose with his mouth. Let me encourage you to be careful of what you say because your words are seeds and your tongue is a sword. Elizabeth was pregnant with John. God had plans for John to prepare the people for Jesus. Therefore, Zechariah's mouth was shut because of his unbelief and position as priest, and with words could have interrupted and John's future purpose.

Fear has consequences. The words that came from Zechariah's mouth were in response to his unbelief, and Gabriel shut his mouth so he wouldn't assassinate the message. Sometimes, we have to shut our own mouths or listen when someone else tells us to shut our mouths. You have to pay attention when God is working and moving in your life. Have you ever been in a situation and if you had just been quiet the circumstances wouldn't have escalated? Fear, anger, bitterness, and unexpectedness will keep you from celebrating yourself and others.

God intervened and closed Zechariah's mouth. Fear will keep you from experiencing the additions God is ready to place in your life. Therefore, walking in the spirit of expectations includes trusting and communicating with God. Plugging into worship, prayer, and fasting in exchange for new expectations includes giving yourself to God and chasing after Him. While Zechariah's voice was gone, he learned new ways to seek God and communicate with Elizabeth. Have situations and experiences transitioned in the way you seek God? Your faith in God needs to continue even if the situation looks barren. Have faith the size of a mustard seed. Do not doubt or put limits on God. Trust God as you begin to transition to take care of yourself and family to understand your Jeremiah 29:11 plans. Remember, God's Word will be revealed and come true at the proper time.

Lesson 6: The crowd is watching. There are people in your crowd who will notice the change(s) in your life. Your crowd will crowd you or crown you. According to Luke 1:21-23, the some people from the crowd stayed for church and others were distracted by Zechariah's silence. As for Zechariah, he soon realized that that he couldn't speak but he could be interpreted (*his gestures that he must have seen a vision in the Temple sanctuary (Luke 1:22). (23) He stayed at the Temple until his term of service was over, and then he returned home.* This was not church service as usual for the worshipers. Imagine how this congregation was feeling while watching Zechariah inside the temple. The plans and purpose God has ready for you requires faith action such as trust and believing in God's plan. The scriptures do not reveal if Zechariah and Elizabeth stopped praying for a child together. Also, the scriptures do not reveal if they physically stopped trying to have a baby, but they prayed for a child. They received their answer and Jeremiah 29:11 plans for John. Gabriel told Zechariah the Jeremiah 29:11 plans for their future son.

Lesson 7:   Zechariah endured silence to the end by being obedient and saying John's name. God opened his mouth when it was time to reveal the name. Let me encourage you to be a champion and persevere through your situation by seeking God's mercy. Always be ready to respond in faith to the plans God has for you. God is not finished with you yet. God hears your prayer petitions.

When it's God's time, your prayers and Jeremiah 29:11 plans will come to pass. It does not matter how old or young you are, God will use you according to His purpose. Fear and doubt will keep you from hearing and receiving the Jeremiah 29:11 plans God has for you. Keep an open mind and heart to receive from God. Be a champion when your plans get interrupted. The plans God has for you will cause you to come out of your comfort zone. Therefore, operate in the spirits of love, peace, and joy. Remember to believe your prayers are being manifested and trust God even when you don't understand the plans.

Still Point Moment: Let me encourage you to keep the faith when your situation gets challenging. Increase your trust range this season as you walk by faith and not by what your situation looks like. This season, do not allow fear to keep you hostage from the Jeremiah 29:11 plans for you.

Still Transition Affirmations: I am a new person in Christ. *Don't copy the behavior and customs of this world, but let God transform you into a new person by changing the way you think (Romans 12:2).*

God's Plan for Man: Forgive

Don't let un-forgiveness block you from your victory. This means you have to operate in the spirit of forgiveness. Forgiveness is written in the Jeremiah 29:11 plans for you. This section is written for you to forgive yourself and others in your assignment. When you operate in forgiveness, you free yourself to be a blessing to the people who trespass against you. Faith without works is dead (James 2:17). Therefore, you have to work in your Jeremiah 29:11 assignment, because your faith will get challenged. Be encouraged as you read this section about forgiveness. It takes this principle to work in your Jeremiah 29:11 assignments. The objective is for you to know that your faith has an assignment. As you continue to read, be still as you discover your Jeremiah 29:11 identities.

Still Point: *May we shout for joy when we hear of your victory, flying banners to honor our God. May the Lord answer all your prayers (Psalm 20:5).*

Jacob's Blessing Becomes Joseph's Favor

(Genesis 37:1) So Jacob settled again in the land of Canaan, where his father had lived. (2) This is the history of Jacob's family. When Joseph was seventeen years old, he often tended his father's flocks with his half-brothers, the sons of his father's wives Bilhah and Zilpah. But Joseph reported to his father some of the bad things his brothers were doing. (3) Now Jacob loved Joseph more than any of his other children because Joseph had been born to him in his old age. So one day he gave Joseph a special gift, a beautiful robe. (4) But his brothers hated Joseph because of their father's partiality. They couldn't say a kind word to him.

Joseph was the firstborn to Rachel, Jacob's second wife. Joseph, Jacob's youngest, was more favored among his twelve sons. Genesis chapter 37, described Joseph as a seventeen-year with a responsible and man-like character *who would report to his father when his half-brothers did bad things* (Genesis 37: 1-4). Joseph's character was different than his brothers. The relationship between

Joseph and Jacob made his brothers jealous. Also, Joseph's gifts and talents were blooming before his maturity. When Joseph was seventeen years old, he often tended his father's flocks with his half-brothers, the sons of his father's wives Leah, Bihah, and Zilpah. Jacob had confidence in Joseph and rewarded him because he was teachable and reliable. It appears that Joseph wanted to be near his father and become like him. However, Jacob knew the Lord was with his sons, especially Joseph.

One day Jacob designed and gave Joseph a colorful robe. The robe is described as a special gift to Joseph. I can imagine Joseph proudly wearing his new robe, while his half-brothers were jealous of the gift. Historically, Jacob's oldest son, Rueben, would have received this robe because of his birth-right. However, Jacob had a different perspective about birth-rights. Jacob's experience from deceiving his father, Isaac, for the birth-right that belonged to Esau had significances in his perspectives and parenting relations. Jacob's older sons were clearly aware that maybe their inheritance could be in jeopardy since Joseph was openly blessed and favored.

You have a similar robe in the Jeremiah 29:11 plans for you. The significance of the robe illustrates that your Heavenly Father has already covered you with grace to fulfill your purpose. God creatively and wonderfully made you in His image and tagged you with purpose to live. Joseph and Jacob have a unique father and son relationship. Your relationship with your Heavenly Father will be revealed as you seek a relationship with Him. God sends His favor to those who seek Him.

Joseph began to dream (Genesis 37: 5-11). I believe that Jacob could relate to his son Joseph because of his faith and relationship with God. Later on, Joseph had two dreams that he shared with his brothers (Genesis 37:5-6; 9-11). Jacob heard Joseph's second dream, and he rebuked him (Genesis 37:10). However Jacob gave Joseph's dream some thought and wondered what it meant (Genesis 37:11).

Jacob was the father of peace and made treaties with his family members and neighbors. Jacob and Joseph had a relationship to which the other brothers could not relate. Jacob's older sons had pervious encounters such as crossed boundaries and bumps along the way of their father and son relationships. For example, Joseph's other brothers destroyed a city when their sister Dina was raped. Also, Rueben slept with one of his father's concubines. Their rebellion against their father broke the treaties Jacob made with other cities. Also, it divided them from Joseph through bitterness, hate, and jealousy.

Jacob knew that he could rely on Joseph to check on his half-brothers while they were at work, so one day he sent him to see about them. Integrity is important in relationships. This is why it is important to consistently give your children chores and educational projects at home. This work ethic is an important principle in the plans God has for you.

One day when Joseph checked on his brothers while at work, they made plans to kill him (Genesis 37:18). Instead, Joseph's brothers physically removed his robe and threw him into a deep pit (Genesis 37:23). Can you imagine how Joseph felt when his brothers pulled off his beautiful robe and threw him in the pit (Genesis 37:23)?

Pit Purpose!

Joseph was thrown in a deep and dark pit. I can imagine that when Joseph was rescued from the pit, he thought he was going back home. However, he was immediately sold into slavery. Suddenly, Joseph was chained and taken away from his familiar home and place. I can imagine Joseph wishing he could have reconciled with his brothers before they made their ultimate decision. Can you imagine Joseph's journey to Egypt? How do you think he coped with his loss of freedom? I believe Joseph talked to God and God spoke to him on his journey to Egypt. As for Joseph, Egypt was a foreign world where he was far from his family was alone from his family for the first time. I truly believe Joseph held on to Jacobs' teachings about the Lord to overcome plots set up against him.

God had a purpose for Joseph and Egypt. Joseph spent his early adulthood years in Egypt as a slave. According to Psalm 105:16, *God called for a famine on the land of Canaan, cutting off its food supply. (17) Then he sent someone to Egypt ahead of them-Joseph, who was sold as a slave. (18) There in prison, they bruised his feet with fetters and placed his neck in an iron collar. (19) Until the time came to fulfill his word, the Lord tested Joseph's character.*

You may feel like you are in a pit. Your pit has a purpose. You may not understand your Jeremiah 29:11 plans because you may be the first one in your family to leave a familiar place. Be encouraged, because you may feel alone and separated from your family but God has plans for you. You may be the first to leave a familiar place and conveniences to get focused about the plans God has for you. The Lord was with Joseph (Genesis 39:2-:21) and he blessed him while he served Potiphar. For example, while a slave, Joseph had been given favor to be in charge. Joseph received Potiphar's favor to be in charge of his house and fields. Let me encourage you that the Lord is with you in every situation. People will notice your gifts and talents especially if you're giving 110% and they are giving 50% to the same work assignments. God's favor will add to your spiritual-fruit, gifts and talents to complete difficult tasks and assignments. Understand that God will be revealed in your life. This means that God will be strong, where you are weak. Therefore, you have to give God the glory in every situation.

Potiphar trusted Joseph's administrative charge and had no worries when he left him in charge to manage many assignments and people. Joseph's teachings and skills learned from his parents were displayed as he served Potiphar. Joseph knew how to serve Potiphar because he respected and was obedient to his father Jacob. Potiphar recognized something different about Joseph because God's favor was with him. Joseph was a champion because he knew his identity and had hope in his situation.

Potiphar's wife noticed Joseph in a different way. Potiphar's wife had personal intentions for Joseph. However Joseph had no interest and was smart enough not to fall into her traps. After Joseph rejected her offer, she made a plan to retaliate. Potiphar's wife accused Joseph of rape with her screams and used his shirt as evidence to create a lie. Then she accused Potiphar of putting her in danger by stating, "That Hebrew slave you've had around here tried to make a fool of me." She used Joseph's Hebrew identity and status as a slave to convince Potiphar that such a person would commit a crime. I believe deep down Potiphar did not believe his wife's claim about Joseph.

Have you been in a situation similar to Joseph's pit experience or became a victim of someone's lies? Did someone's false claims cause you to lose a position? How did you respond to their false claims? Potiphar's response to his enraged thoughts was to put Joseph out of sight, which was in prison with a difference position and charge. However, Potiphar knew Joseph was innocent. I believe Joseph was tired of being a prisoner and being told what to do. Joseph was in a prison in the palace of Potiphar. Potiphar assigned Joseph to take care of Pharaoh's chief cupbearer and chief baker.

Your Gift's Assignment

Sometime later, Pharaoh's chief cupbearer and chief baker offended him (Genesis 40:1). (2) Pharaoh became very angry with these officials, (3) and he put them in the prison where Joseph was, in the palace of Potiphar, the captain of the guard. (4) They remained in prison for quite some time, and Potiphar assigned Joseph to take care of them. (5) One day the cupbearer and the baker each had a dream, and each dream had its own meaning. (6) The next morning Joseph noticed the dejected look on their faces. (7) "Why do you look so worried today?" he asked. (8) And they both replied, "We both had dreams last night, but there is no one here to tell us what they mean." "Interpreting dreams is God's business," Joseph replied, "Tell me what you saw." Both explained to Joseph their dreams, and he interpreted their dreams to them (Genesis 40:9-19). Joseph asked the cupbearer to have some pity on him when he returns back to Pharaoh, however he promptly forgot all about Joseph, never giving him another thought (Genesis 40:23).

Your gift is always on assignment to bless others. I believe Joseph was tired of living as a prisoner. But Joseph knew God had plans for him because his gifts and extraordinary work ethics were phenomenal. Have you ever been in a place that you wanted to get out? Have you helped others in their time of need? How did they return your favor? God's grace and favor is shining over your life as you began to overcome situations.

Remember, your gift is designed to help someone else. Potiphar assigned Joseph to take care of them (Genesis 40:4) and used his gift to interpret the dreams of these prisoners. Your gifts are always on assignment to bless someone in their time of need. Remember that your gifts comes from God and He has strategically designed your gifts to bless others, as well as you. For example, from the day Joseph was put in charge, the Lord began to bless Potiphar for Joseph's sake. All his household affairs began to run smoothly, and his crops and livestock flourished (Genesis 39: 5). Let me encourage you that you can receive a blessing through helping and encouraging others. In the struggle and captivity, Joseph remained hopeful.

Two years later, Pharaoh had dreams (Genesis 41:1-7) that needed to be interpreted. After having these dreams, he called for all the magicians and wise men of Egypt and told them about his dreams, but not one of them could suggest what they meant (Genesis 41:8). (9) Then the king's cupbearer spoke up. "Today I have been reminded of my failure," he said. Here is when the cupbearer used this opportunity to remind Pharaoh where he placed him and the chief baker, and met Joseph. He tells Pharaoh how Joseph (12) told them what each of their dreams meant, (13) and everything happened just as he said it would. (14) Pharaoh sent for Joseph at once, and he was brought hastily from the dungeon. After a quick shave and change of clothes, he went in and stood in Pharaoh's presence. (15) "I had a dream last night," Pharaoh told him, "and none of these men can tell me what it means. But I have heard that you can interpret dreams, and that is why I have called for you." (16) "It is beyond my power to do this," Joseph replied. "But God will tell you what it means and will set you at ease." (17) So Pharaoh told him the dream. (Genesis 41: 17-25). Joseph tells Pharaoh his suggestions and plans to prepare for the disaster (Genesis 41:33-36). After consideration, Pharaoh said, (39) "Since God has revealed the meaning of the dreams to you, you are the wisest man in the land. (40) I hereby appoint you to direct this project. You will manage my household and organize all my people. Only I will have rank higher than yours.

At an early age, Joseph knew there was purpose in his life. Pharaoh, Potiphar, and the chief jailer had no worries when Joseph was in the fields, in the prison, or in the palace working. Your purpose has an appointment. The combinations of your past, people, and experiences have prepared you for to your purpose. Your setbacks are part of your Jeremiah 29:11 plans. Your purposes have appointments. Therefore, it is time for you to get out of the pit.

Are you the same person now out of the pit, than you were in the pit? What did you learn while you were in the pit? Who were you serving to get out of the pit? Did you clothes change? Did your name change? Did your mind get renewed? Do your haters recognize you now that you're out of the pit? Do you look like the hell you were thrown into?

The new Joseph had grown up and was now governor of Egypt. You are a new person in Christ (II Corinthians 5:17) once you let go and forgive. Your gift is always on assignment to get you out of the pit, carry you through the hard times, and bless others in their times of need. Joseph's experiences and promotions were part of the plans God had for him, the regions around Egypt, and future generations. Let me encourage you not to have pity in the pit. Your gifts are designed to get you out of the pit. Looking back, Joseph learned how to serve Potiphar from his personal relationship with his father Jacob.

As you seek a relationship with the Heavenly Father, you can prepare you and your family for their Jeremiah 29:11 assignments. Men can plant the Word of God in lives of children in the position as a coach, facilitator, advocate, and teachers. In these positions, Men of God, can help the children recognize that God has plans for them. Your responsibility is to cover them in prayer as they go about the Father's business. The results of early bonds and attachment can establish health relationships between the child and the father. The love and teachings that Joseph experienced from his father Jacob helped him survive in the pit and in slavery.

The only time Joseph asked for pity was after he interpreted the dreams of the cup-bearer and the baker (Genesis 40:13). Joseph remained obedient while getting sold into slavery, serving Potiphar in the field, being accused of rape, ending up in prison, and becoming second in command in Egypt. Joseph operated in his gifts to serve and forgive. He kept his relationship with His God as the primary focus in every ordeal. Consequently, he was able to come out of slavery and prison. Joseph's work ethic allowed him to see value instead of playing the victim. Your gift is designed to counsel, carry a message, prepare someone for a change, or give someone hope in a famine. Freedom comes when you forgive others.

(Genesis 45:4) "I am Joseph, your brother whom you sold into Egypt. (5) But don't be angry with yourselves that you did this to me, for God did it. He sent me here ahead of you to preserve your lives. (6) These two years of famine will grow to seven, during which there will be neither plowing nor harvest. (7) God has sent me here to keep you and your families alive so that you will become a great nation. (8) Yes, it was God who sent me here, not you! And he has made me a counselor to Pharaoh, manager of his entire household and ruler over all Egypt. (17) Pharaoh said to Joseph, "Tell your brothers to load their pack animals and return quickly to their homes in Canaan. (18) Tell them to bring your father and all of their families, and to come here to Egypt to live. Tell them 'Pharaoh will assign to you the best territory in the land of Egypt. You will live off the fat of the land!' (19) And tell our brothers to take wagons from Egypt to carry their wives and little ones and to bring your father here. (20) Don't worry about your belongings, for the best of all the land of Egypt is yours."

Joseph's gifts of forgiveness and blessings made room enough for his brothers, fathers, and future generations to survive during a famine. Pharaoh provided wagons to help make their travel transition to live in Egypt and eat. There are many lessons to be learned from Joseph.

1. Wear your robe. The plans God has for you fits you.
2. Forgive. Operate in forgiveness with those who hurt and plot against you.
3. Your gifts are designed to bless others.
4. Your gifts are designed to get you out the pit.
5. Your gifts are designed for God to be revealed.
6. In the plans God has for you, God will never abandon you.

7. The plans God has for you will mature you and prepare you for your purpose.

Be a champion and wear your Jeremiah 29:11 royal robes from your Heavenly Father. This season walk with in the Jeremiah 29:11 plans and purposes. You best is yet to come in your purposes.

Still Point Moment: Joseph wore many robes in his life. These robes illustrate how he managed his gifts and talents from God while in the pit, prison, and palace. In the plans God has for you, the plans are designed for you to have hope even when you have been betrayed or pushed into a pit. Joseph used his gifts to interpret dreams and talents to serve and forgive others. His gifts and talents gave him favor in the eyes of Potiphar and Pharaoh. God has given you a robe to wear in your Jeremiah 29:11 assignments. This means that you are covered as you continue to walk in the plans God has for you.

Still Transition Affirmations: *Not that I was ever in need, for I have learned how to get along happily whether I have much or little (Philippians 4:11).* As you move forward on your Jeremiah 29:11 journey keep in mind these tips for success as they relate to transition: be self-directed, resourceful, and proactive.

Section Three:
Have Faith Still Point Section Reflection

In this section, Joseph and Zechariah were alone for a period of time. You may experience times in your life when you are alone. However, it is important for you to have faith in times you are alone. It's during your alone time when you can process and hear from God.

You cannot remain the way you are. You may be experiencing a phase known as transition. In this transition, you are being God-prep to receive and be planted in the plans God has for you. Trust God in your seasons of changes. Let go of the things, people, and places that hinder your peace and blessings. Let me encourage you to hold on to the Word of God. Believe in the Word of God and shout with an advance praise.

Let me encourage you to know that your gifts are designed to get you out of the pit and challenges you may face. God will give you the strength to endure any situation and his glory will be revealed. Remember that the pit is a temporary place. Blaming others and feeling sorry for yourself are traps set by the enemy to trap keep you stuck. There is a newer you waiting for you! Operate in forgiveness and faith in the plans God has for you. God will be revealed and you will get the victory. As you transition from your one place to another, hold on to your dreams and teachings from your Heavenly Father.

Section Four:
Be Champions

God's Plan for Man: Be the Head of Your Generation

Your victories today set the next generation to operate and towards building the Kingdom of God. You must confront and conquer situations that challenge you. The next generations are counting on you to fight the good fight and conquer in the places that belong to God. This means you have to operate in as a victor and be the head of your generation. Being the head of your generation is written in the Jeremiah 29:11 plans for you. This section is written for you to be a victor and not a victim in your assignment. Be encouraged as you read these this section, "Be the head of your generation." It takes the principles of commitment, responsibilities, and work to get the job done in your Jeremiah 29:11 assignments. The objective is to know that your faith has an assignment. As you continue to read, be still as you discover your Jeremiah 29:11 identities.

Still Point: *My God, my God! Why have you forsaken me? Why do you remain so distant? Why do you ignore my cries for help (Psalm 22:1)?*

You may be the first person in your family to move away from a familiar place and move your family to a new region. Joseph fulfilled the plans God had for Abraham's successors.

Your Legacy

(Exodus 1:6) In time, Joseph and each of his brothers died, ending that generation. (1) These are the sons of Jacob who went with their father to Egypt, each with his family. (2) Reuben, Simeon, Levi, Judah, (3) Issachar, Zebulun, Benjamin, (4) Dan, Naphtali, Gad, and Asher. (5) Joseph was already down in Egypt. In all, Jacob had seventy direct descendants. (7) But their descendants had many

children and grandchildren. In fact, they multiplied so quickly that they soon filled the land. (8) Then a new king came to the throne of Egypt who knew nothing about Joseph or what he had done.

During this season, Joseph and his brothers died. Jacob's descendants multiplied and kept their Israelite identity. The descendants of the Twelve Tribes multiplied in the land of Egypt as slaves. A new king was on the throne who knew nothing about Joseph's leadership over Egypt. Where did this king come from? Why was he unaware of Joseph's success? While enslaved, the Israelites remain fruitful and multiplied.

Pharaoh put Joseph in charge of the entire Egypt (Genesis 41:41). (42) Pharaoh placed his own signet ring on Joseph's finger as a symbol of his authority. He dressed him in beautiful clothing and placed the royal gold chain about his neck. (43) Pharaoh also gave Joseph the chariot of his second-in-command, and wherever he went the command was shouted, "Kneel down!" So Joseph was put in charge of all Egypt. (44) And Pharaoh said to Joseph, "I am the king, but no one will move a hand or foot in the entire land of Egypt without your approval."

It is important to leave an inheritance for your children and so on. In his position as governor, Joseph said to his brothers, *(Genesis 50:24) "Soon I will die, but God will surely come for you, to lead you out of this land of Egypt. He will bring you back to the land he vowed to give to the descendants of Abraham, Isaac, and Jacob."* Without knowing, this new king was only focused on killing Joseph's dreams and the nation of Israel's promise by making the Israelites slaves.

Why didn't the new king receive an orientation to the historical and geographical innovations Joseph left behind? The book of Genesis reveals that a new king knew nothing about Joseph or what he had done. Let me encourage you about the importance of your Jeremiah 29:11 plans. It is important that you share the Word of God, teachings, and values to your children and so on. Also, it is important to teach the current generation to build up the Kingdom of God on Earth and discover their Jeremiah 29:11 plans. The plans of the new king were to oppress the Hebrews. The leaders and priest of the

Hebrews were aware of the oppression; however, they did not counterattack the conditions. Instead, the leaders and Israelites accepted their culture and lifestyle as slaves. My brothers, if you tolerate a situation too long, it won't change. You need to consider how today's actions will affect tomorrow's generation. Therefore, as a leader you need to have a relationship and know the people you are leading. The people you are leading need responsibilities and trainings to understand their assignments.

The Israelites were the generations beginning with Abraham's promise, Isaac's blessing, and Jacob's sons multiplying as the twelve tribes. The descendants of the twelve tribes were robbed of the land in which Joseph was sold into slavery and later became second in charge of all Egypt (Genesis 41: 43). These generations were robbed of their freedom. As the Israelites multiplied, they continued to praise, pray, and worship God while in slavery. During the oppression, the Israelites were still multiplying and giving birth. During their slavery, they remained faithful to their promise, blessing, by multiplying and birthing their purpose. However, every newborn boy faced the threat of death at birth.

The principles of work and responsibly are important in the plans God has for you. It is important to leave wealth, business, homes, and land for your children and family. Most of all, it is important to set your children to own land and not live as foreigners in areas they do not know. Therefore, it is important to train your children in the ways of the Lord and help other families needing help. These responsibilities include teaching your children your family identity and history. It is important to share and celebrate with your children any educational and career achievements of your family members. Be a champion and help your elders and younger generations. Children need to know and see relevant examples through their family and community members. Understand that you have a responsibility to have success and leave a legacy for your family and community.

Still Point Moment: You need to teach traditions and the ways of the Lord to your children. Get ready to finish the projects you started and leave a legacy. The generations after you need to be taught the values and principles of God to live in their Jeremiah 29:11

assignments. Let me encourage and remind you to record your family history and achievements in education and careers. Give back to your family and community by being a bridge between the older and younger generations. Your involvement may help build awareness of your family and community history and achievements; which can Jeremiah 29:11 legacy for the next generations.

Still Transition Affirmations: God is with me. *If God be for us, who can ever be against us (Romans 8:31b).*

God's Plan for Man: Confront It!

You have to confront a situation if you want to conquer it. God is equipping you for your Jeremiah 29:11 appointment. You are in the in-between time of your today and promise. This means that you have to pray, wait, and be still for your answer about how to confront and conquer. Also, you can work at building your faith and aligning yourself to the promises of God. The skills to confront and conquer are written in the Jeremiah 29:11 plans for you. This section is written for you to confront and conquer in your assignment. Be encouraged as you read this section, "Confront it! Conquer it!" It takes these principles to work in your Jeremiah 29:11 assignments. The objective is to know that your faith has an assignment. As you continue to read, be still as you discover your Jeremiah 29:11 identities.

Still Point: *Victory comes from you, O Lord. May your blessings rest on your people (Psalms 3:8).*

Your Plans Will Get Challenged, But Keep Your Faith

This section is to encourage you that God has plans for you. God has plans for children. David was Jesse's youngest son. He worked in Jesse's field as a shepherd (1Samuel 16:11). Be encouraged and hold on to your faith as you cultivate your ground to harvest the Jeremiah 29:11 plans for you! People draw their impressions of you based on your height, size, gender, and race. Sometimes people make their impressions based on what they think you can do. Does their opinion of you matter? How confident are you to ignore what people say? Your gifts will become developed as you go through the process and prepare for your Jeremiah 29:11 assignments.

Let me encourage you to hear, read, and know what the Word of God says about you. In the plans God has for you, you must use your spiritual talents and gifts as shields to defeat and slay giants. The 'fear' factor is not part of *II Timothy 1:7, For God has not given us a spirit of fear and timidity, but of power, love, and self.* You can overcome any challenge that appears to cause anxiety. Let me encourage you to make room in your heart for the Jeremiah 29:11 plans to have hope and prosper in the Lord. In the plans God has for you victory is included. Let me encourage you to be a champion and stand on II Timothy 1:7 as you step on defeat, fear, deception, anxiety, and depression. The enemy's army may try to fight against you, invade your land, and challenge you but God has given you the victory over any challenge.

You are a champion because God chose you according to His purpose. David was the youngest of his brothers. At the time Samuel anointed David, King Saul lost God's favor to govern Israel. Samuel followed God's instruction to anoint one of Jesse's sons as king. Jesse had sons in Saul's army, but God choose David. At a young age, David had a good reputation as a shepherd and musician. God had plans for Israel's future with David as the king. God has plans for you while you are in the process of transition. He is making and shaping you for your divine role. Let me encourage you to keep working in your field and develop your gifts and talents until your appointed time. No matter your past, God can use you. God is watching over the Jeremiah 29:11 seed that is planted within you to complete a good work.

Still Point Moment: You have what it takes to face your situation even while transition. You are equipped when you pray and praise to the Lord. You can get rid of anxiety by getting in the Word more and humbling yourself (II Chronicles 7:14).

Still Transition Affirmations: I have peace. *I am leaving you with a gift-peace of mind and heart. And the peace I give isn't like the peace the word gives. So don't be troubled or afraid (John 14:27).*

God's Plan for Man: Be Champions

God made us to be champions. This is why it is important for us to walk in victory. To be a champion is to use God's principles to work in your Jeremiah 29:11 assignments. The objective is to know that your faith has an assignment.

Still Point: *Surely your goodness and unfailing love will pursue me all the days of my life, and I will live in the house of the Lord forever (Psalm 23:6).*

David's life story is phenomonal. David can be described as a champion, suceessful military commander, father, husband, and king. He had many positions throughout his life. Victory comes when you allow God to fight your battles and the reward is a new position. David accepted his responsibilities as a shepherd and musician when he was young. Since David was Jesse's youngest son, I can imagine him diligently waking up early to complete his shepherd duties in order to be on time at the palace. David was aware of his responsibilities and the importance to finish his work. David's life reflects his discipleship, relationship, and worship with God. God is revealed throughout David's life.

Your Field Has a Purpose

As a child, David was in the fields with a responsibility to shepherd his father's sheep. The sheep pastures were David's training ground to develop his musical gifts and military strategies. David became the sheep's provider for food and protection. The sheep listened to his voice and music. I can imagine in the mornings when David woke up and headed to the fields. David would begin to play his harp which would draw the sheep to him. The harp was part of a routine for the sheep to prepare for their day and for their journey. I imagine the harp was a technique David used for the sheep to follow him and find him. As a shepherd, David had to protect the sheep from predator mountain animals such as bears, wolves, and lions.

David became a skilled warrior and saved his sheep from these predators. Yet, did David know that the pastures were his training ground to worship God, create music with the harp, lead a future army, and become a king?

Jesse, David's father, had a good reputation as a carpenter and father. As David worked in his father's field, and people noticed and heard his music talents. The harp was an instrument David learned how to make and play while in the fields with the sheep. David played this instrument to worship the Lord with psalms and praise.

(I Samuel 16:14) the Spirit of the Lord has left Saul, and the Lord sent a tormenting spirit that filled him with depression and fear. (15) Some of Saul's servants suggested a remedy. "It is clear that a spirit from God is tormenting you, "they said. (16) "Let us find a good musician to play the harp for you whenever the tormenting spirit is bothering you. The harp music will quiet you, and you will soon be well again."(18) One of the servants said to Saul, "The son of Jesse is a talented harp player. Not only that; he is brave and strong and has good judgment. He is also a fine-looking young man, and the Lord is with him." (19) So Saul, sent messengers to Jesse to say, "Send me your son David to Saul, along with a young goat and a donkey loaded down with food and wine. (21) So David went to Saul and served him, and David became one of Saul's armor bearers? (22) Then Saul set word to Jesse asking, "Please let David join my staff, for I am very pleased with him" (23) And whenever the tormenting spirit from God troubled Saul, David would play the harp. Then Saul would feel better, and the tormenting spirit would go away.

Have you ever been recommended for an employment or appointed to a leadership position? If so, how did your experience promote or terminate your employment? Man of God, people are watching you and your gifts unfold. As a father, people are watching how you interact with your children and how you are training them up, as well as how you interact with others. Saul's servant recommended David's because of his character, his music ministry, and his brave reputation of fighting lions and bears to protect his father's sheep. The people you meet are important in the plans God has for you. You don't know who is watching or discovering your unique characteristics. Also, let me encourage you not to remain the way you are as you work in your field. Be a champion and develop your character in the plans God has for you. Be ready, like David, to say, "Yes!" and step into your promotion. Remember that God has people watching you when you think no one is looking.

Crossroads: David and Goliath

David began his music assignment to serve King Saul while continuing his work as a shepherd's boy. *I Samuel 17:15 But David went back and forth between working for Saul and helping his father with the sheep in Bethlehem. While David was traveling between the palace and home, Goliath was challenging the Israelites daily for a fight (I Samuel 17:25).*

Along the way, David had to protect himself between the paths of Jesse's home and the palace. Just as David described God in Psalm *23:4, "Even when I walk through the dark valley of death, I will not be afraid, you are close besides me.* David is speaking about his relationship with God by identifying Him as his Shepherd. David can testify that God's rod and staff protected and comforted him from danger (Psalm 23), as he traveled back and forward between his jobs as a shepherd and musician. He heard and saw the challenges of Goliath, but that never stopped him from getting to work. There are lessons we can learn from David's commitment to his positions. I believe David protected himself with rocks and a sling shot in his side-pouch and a rod in his belt as he traveled between his jobs. I can imagine David carrying his harp in his hand. These protections were how he protected the sheep. Most of all, I can imagine David strategizing how to defeat Goliath. Your crossroads are part of your Jeremiah 29:11 plans to develop your character. Therefore, let me encourage you to have integrity when no one is around or looking. Be ready for your assignments or a challenge while you're in the crossroads.

Jesse's Instructions

I Samuel 17:17, One day Jesse said to David, "Take this half-bushel of roasted grain and these ten loaves of bread to your brothers." (I Samuel 17:20) So David left the sheep with another shepherd and set out early the next morning with the gifts. He arrived at the outskirts of the camp just as the Israelite army was leaving for the battlefield with shout and battle cries. (21) Soon the Israelite and Philistine forces stood facing each other. (22) David left his things with the keeper of supplies and hurried out to the ranks to greet his brothers. (23) As he was talking with them, he saw Goliath the champion from Gath, come out from the Philistine ranks, shouting his challenge to the army of Israel.

Jesse gave David an assignment to meet his brothers at their post. David took the bread to his brothers. Daily, Goliath came out to challenge (I Samuel 17:16) the Israelite Army for a fight. The Israelites and Saul's army saw as well as heard Goliath's challenges daily (I Samuel 17:25) and they would run away in fright (I Samuel 17:24). There is a reward from King Saul to anyone who killed Goliath. In the case of Saul and the Israelite Army, they had been facing the same challenges with the same weapons with no strategy. It appeared that they became regular audience members of the daily 'Goliath Show.' David knew that he did not want to be a spectator. His shepherd and the warrior spirit stirred up on the inside of him to finally face this challenge. Some of us have tried to use the weapons and clothing of others to protect us over and over again. David didn't use Saul's armor because King Saul didn't use his own amour to protect him. David used his gifts to fight Goliath. He used his shepherd boy skills and training to amour up for his fight. We need to amour up today with our weapons, tools, gifts from God. Ephesians 6 states to put on the whole amour.

Face Your Giants

David began to ask again, "what will a man get for killing this Philistine and putting an end to his abuse of Israel?" He asked them, "Who is the pagan Philistine anyway, that he is allowed to defy the armies of the God (26)." And David received the same reply as before: "What you have been hearing is true. That is the reward for killing the giant." (27) And David received the same reply as before, "What you have been hearing is true. That is the reward for killing the giant." (32) Don't worry about a thing," David told Saul, "I'll go fight this Philistine!" 33) Don't be ridiculous!" Saul replied. "There is no way you can go against this Philistine. You are only a boy, and he has been in the army since he was a boy!" 34) But David persisted. "I have been taking care of my father's sheep," he said "When a lion or a bear comes to steal a lamb from the flock, 35) I go after it with a club and take the lamb from its mouth. If the animal turns to me, I catch it by the jaw and club it to death. 36) I have done this to both lions and bears, and I'll do this pagan Philistine, too, for he has defied the armies of the living God! 37) The Lord who saves me from the claws of the lion and bear will save me from this Philistine!" Saul finally consented, "All right go ahead," he said. "And may the Lord be with you!"

Saul limited David because of his size; however David knew God was on his side. Before David's challenge to Goliath, King Saul tried to give David his armor of a bronze element and a coat of mail to wear for the battle (I Samuel 17:38). *(39) David put it on, strapped the sword over it, and took a step or two to see what it was like, for he had never worn such things before. "I can't go in these," he protested. "I'm not used to them." So he took them off again.*

What giants are challenging you daily? Let me encourage you that the armor of the Lord will protect you from the threats and harm from a giant. The people in your crowd may see and hear the same giant and watch you battle by yourself. You may be in this challenge alone, and your family members, church members, and friends may be aware of your situation; however you must trust God and stay in the fields. Do you want your reward? When David arrived at Camp Saul, he could tell it was out of order. Can you imagine an army running away in fright from one giant? I can imagine David was thinking, "Who was the general of this army? Who was the visionary leader of this group?"

Trusting God activates your rewards for confronting the giants that have challenged, threatened, and destroyed the fields designed for you. You receive many gains when you allow God to be God. There is a reward for confronting and conquering the giant that has been challenging you and your family. The reward is God's promotion and appointment. The power of God will be revealed to your enemies. The reward is when you begin to pray for one another and stand corporately against the giant. Only then, can the Word move it out of the way.

Be a champion by putting on the amour of the Lord. Your spiritual weapons are stored in a sling and ready to be used when you lift of the name of God. It's time to be free from any challenges that hinder you. It's time to confront and conquer the giant and receive your reward. It's time to train for the challenge and kill the giant. It's time to conquer fear and face the challenge. Understand that one day you have to face and kill your giant. Your gift will make you a champion over your giant. Let me encourage you that God is not finished with you yet. God has plans for you. Get your mind made up to serve the Lord. God appointed David at a young age, while he worked in his father's field. If you are waiting for God to deliver, have faith that God will answer and full every promise.

Still Point Moment: Take this moment to identify the Goliath(s) that challenge you. You have the weapons to confront and conquer the giants in your mind, journey to work or at work, or in your house. You have the power to conquer it whether it's low self-esteem or addiction to substances, pain medication, caffeine, food, sex, or curse words. What weapons have you considered to fight and resist these daily challenges that are defeating you? Your gifts and talents are designed for you to win over the challenges that face you.

The victory is yours to be the king over the Goliath that is challenging you. What God has created and designed is your gift to conquer any giants (Isaiah 54:17). Greater is He that is in you that he that is in the world. You are a winner! Let me encourage you to continue pressing towards your next level, even if that means asking questions to get to your reward. Continue creating a strategy to get your reward. Victory is yours!

Still Transition Affirmations: I am a worshipper. *Since we are receiving a kingdom that cannot be destroyed, let us be thankful and* *please God by worshipping Him with Holy fear and awe (Hebrew 12:28).*

God's Plans for Man: Know Your Father

Speak to your situation with the word of God. It is imperative that you speak the word of God to your situation. Why? Everything created was spoken and made by God. "Know Your Father" is important to conquer situations in front of you. The Word of God is written in the Jeremiah 29:11 plans for you. This section is written for you to know your Father and understand your assignment. Be encouraged as you read this section, "Know your Father". It takes this principle to work in your Jeremiah 29:11 assignments. The objective is to know that your faith has an assignment as you continue to read.

Still Point: *But they delight in doing everything the Lord wants' day and night they think about his law (Psalm 1:2)*

I Samuel 17 :(46) Today, the Lord will conquer you, and I will kill you and cut off your head. And then I will give the dead bodies of your men to the birds and wild animals, and the whole world will know that there is a God in Israel. (47) And everyone will know that the Lord does not need weapons to rescue his people. It is his battle, not ours; The Lord will give you to us!" (48) As Goliath moved closer to attack, David quickly ran out to meet him. (49) Reaching into his shepherd's bag and taking out a stone, he hurled it from his sling and hit the Philistine in the forehead. The stone sank in, and Goliath stumbled and fell downward to the ground. (50) So David triumphed over the Philistine giant with only a stone and sling. David used it to kill the giant and cut off his head. (57) After David had killed Goliath, Abner brought him to Saul with the Philistine's head still in his hand. (58) "Tell me about your father, my boy," Saul said. And David replied, "His name is Jesse, and we live in Bethlehem."

One stone had a purpose. Everything around you has a purpose to take down strongholds and keep you in your Jeremiah 29:11 purposes. Your weapons are working for you. David's victory over Goliath took place with previous victories and protecting the sheep. David was professional with his weapons against his opponents. People that are around you have motives to either keep you where you are at or take you to your next level. Abner had a purpose to bring David to Saul with Goliath's head. Abner got rid of the head. The head of represents the death of things challenging you. The things and people you confront head-on will not challenge you no more. The things you are experiencing are making you better and stronger in the Jeremiah 29:11 plans for you. Your victories are helping present and future generations get to their next levels.

David's courage revealed his relationship with God. God used David supernaturally in the challenge, and wants to use you. Your role as a father is critical in the spiritual identity in the Jeremiah 29:11 plans God has for you and your children. Therefore, it is important for you to know your Heavenly Father in order to understand your Jeremiah 29:11 assignments. Pray this season to think of yourself as a champion. You may be going through a transition; however, let go of the things and people God is removing from your world. Let me encourage your to have a re-new mind through a relationship with God.

Giants

Today's victories lead to tomorrow's victories. The Israelites continued to encounter war against the Philistines and giants while David was the king according to II Samuel 21:17-20.

II Samuel 21:17 Abishai son of Zeruiah killed Ishbi-Benob

II Samuel 21:18 Sibbekai the Hushathite killed Saph

II Samuel 21:19 Elhanan son of Jair killed the brother of Goliath the Gittite.

II Samuel 21:20 Jonathan son of Shimeah (David's brother) killed the Rapha Giant with six fingers on each hand and six toes on each foot.

II Samuel 21:22 These four were descendants of Rapha in Gath, and they fell at the hands of David and his men.

King David was able to face the giants because he had a relationship with his earthly and Heavenly Father. Also, King David had experience and victory against the giant Goliath because of his field experiences as a shepherd and working as a musician for King Saul. The Israelites and Saul's Army were witnesses to David's victory and previous work ethics. Therefore, King David trained his officers with the same military skills to defeat the next giants or enemies challenging them. It's important to confront the situations challenging your family, community, and nation. Most importantly it is important to fight with a strategy. The enemy is always on duty to steal, kill, and destroy your victory. Goliath's family wanted revenge. Watch out for people with plan for revenge. People with revenge in mind want justice their way, especially if they are losing.

I can imagine the Israelites' faith and confidence levels increasing as they began to witness the end of the Rapha giants. Your children are watching how you defeat the giants challenging your surroundings. They are taking notes how to approach situations that affect them with their peers and teachers at school, part-time jobs, or places where they volunteer. It is important to support your children now because as they grow older, they will give wise advice to their generation.

Reflections of Jesse

After David's victory over Goliath, King Saul was interested in knowing about David's father. David proudly told King Saul his father's name. Generally, people want to know the children's family connections when they are succeeding. However, King Saul had known David as his musician without making family connections to Jesse and his brothers.

Jesse knew that David was anointed to become a king, but he didn't know when it was going to happen. Jesse was aware of David's strengths and weakness which is why he agreed for David to work in the palace when Saul was tormented with spirits. He felt peace when David was walking between home and the palace. David's gift positioned him inside the palace as one of Saul's messengers. Jesse believed and David in the palace as Saul's musician in obedience and as a response to God sending Samuel to anoint David as king. Jesse was obedient to God's assignment and plans for his son, David. Below is some history of his lineage;

1. He was the father of eight sons (three sons joined Saul's army-Eliab, Abinadab, and Shamah , I Samuel 16:13)
2. David, the youngest was anointed as king (I Samuel 16:13)
3. He gave his sons a field and sheep to watch (16:11)
4. He allowed Samuel to perform the purification rite for Jesse and his sons (I Samuel 16:5)
5. He believed Samuel when he said, *"The Lord has not chosen any of these (I Samuel 16:12-13)."*
6. Jesse believed and sent for David, and he was the one to be anointed.

Given this rich heritage, ask yourself these questions:

What is your parental resume?

What are you feeding to your children?

What are your parenting tools to make warriors for the army of the Lord?

What are your children saying about you?

What have you sown in your children's field for their future?

How are you training them up for the Goliaths? Bears? Lions?

What weapons are you training them to use for the battle?

Are you training up your children to hear the Shepherd's voice in the field?

Are you teaching them how to worship in their field?

Still Point Moment: God is not finished with you yet. Be encouraged and support your children as they grow and mature as soldiers in their Jeremiah 29:11 purposes. What are your children saying about you? How are they describing your parenting to others? How are they demonstrating your teachings and training? Can you picture and hear David bragging on his father, Jesse? Can you imagine Jesse praising and praying to God to prepare his son to become a king? Can you imagine their conversations and prayer life? Can you imagine Jesse showing David how to use a club to fight and protect the sheep from thieves and animal predators?

Still Transition Affirmations: I am a champion in Christ. *And you will know the truth, and the truth will set you free (John 8:32).* As you move forward on your Jeremiah 29:11 journey keep in mind these tips for success as they relate to transition: be self-directed, resourceful, and proactive.

Section Four Reflection:
Be Champions

Work and responsibly are principles that are important in the plans God has for you. Therefore, it is important to set the work ethic and example to your children in the ways of the Lord. David had work and responsibility ethics that developed him from a shepherd in his father's field, promoted to King Saul's musician, and skilled giant slayer. Later, his work and responsibility ethic grew into his leadership role as a king and warrior. David was brave and courageous and confronted his issues. You have to confront the situation if you want to conquer it. While you are going through your God-prep, you have to pray, wait, and be still for your answer how to confront and conquer. There are going to be people in your Jeremiah 29:11 path that will give you assignments. These assignments are designed to develop your character and maturity to walk you to your next Jeremiah 29:11 levels. This is important in the role of the father to train your children according to Proverbs 22:6. You are raising sons and daughters to become champions in the Kingdom of God. Therefore; it is important to understand your strengths and weaknesses in your assignments. Understand that God will be strong where you are weak when you're operating in your Jeremiah 29:11 plans. Your field assignment will help you grow and mature in to your new level and assignment. Keep your faith because your field assignments are getting you ready for your Jeremiah 29:11 purpose and identity.

Section Five:
The Ministry of Fatherhood

God's Plan for Man: Be Your Brother's Keeper

There are all kinds of people in your life. However, there are those with good intentions to help you with no strings attached. People with good intentions want to see you go to your next level in God. "Be Your Brother's Keeper" is written in the Jeremiah 29:11 plans for you. This section is written for you to resist competition and be a helper to others in their Jeremiah 29:11 assignments. Be encouraged as you read this section about be your brother's keeper. It takes this principle to work in your Jeremiah 29:11 assignments. The objective is to know that your faith has an assignment to help somebody else.

Still Point: *I will praise you, Lord, ore you have rescued me. You refused to let my enemies triumph over me (Psalm 30:1).*

I Samuel 18:1, After David had finished talking with Saul; he met Jonathan, the king's son. There was an immediate bond of love between them, and they became the best of friends. (2) From that day on Saul kept David with him at the palace and wouldn't let him return home. (3) And Jonathan made a special vow to be David's friend, (4) and he sealed the pact by giving him his robe, tunic, sword, bow, and belt.

The responsibility of being a father includes thinking about your own and other children. This role is stretched to a brother, uncle, neighbor, mentor, teacher, and friend. David heart sought after God. His actions were different because of his relationship with God. David and Saul's son Jonathan shared a common brotherhood. Jonathan's kindness towards David to be his brother and not an enemy was demonstrated in his vow and gifts such as a robe, tunic, sword, bow, and belt for a prince. Jonathan honored David for his victory against Goliath and new position as King. Jonathan and David had a special brotherhood that included a vow. This vow represented a Godly covenant and foundation to Mephibosheth's tides to royalty. This royalty is connected to the Abrahamic covenant which is God's promise to make Abraham the father of many great nations, bless those who bless him, and curse those who curse him. The Holy Spirit is working in you to help you obey God and know your Jeremiah 29:11 purposes, plans, and identities. David and Jonathan had many victories together as soldiers in the army of the Lord. Jonathan had a son named Mephibosheth. One day on the battlefield, King Saul and Prince Jonathan lost their lives. In an instant, Mephibosheth's familiar residence, home, and people became a memory.

Mephibosheth did not know about the vow his father made, but David remembered. Remember the promises that you've made to others. David was loyal to his promises as je one day wondered if anyone in Saul's family was still alive (II Samuel 9:1). David asked for a man named Ziba who was one of Saul's servants. Ziba answered King David's question and said that Mephibosheth was alive. David wanted to show kindness to Mephibosheth who was Jonathan's son and Saul's grandson (II Samuel 9:6). The Bible doesn't reveal that Mephibosheth's prayed or asked for help, but help came through King David.

And from that time on, Mephibosheth ate regularly with David, as though he were one of his own sons (II Samuel 9:11b).(12) Mephibosheth had a young son named Mica. And from then on, all the members of Ziba's household were Mephibosheth's servants. (13)And Mephibosheth, who was crippled in both feet, moved to Jerusalem to live at the palace (II Samuel 9:13).

In an instant Mephibosheth's life was changed. He and his family left the place of Lo-debar and moved to Jerusalem. Let me encourage you to bless someone and help your family members get on their feet. David appointed and showed kindness to Mephibosheth by giving him his inheritance which was all the land that once belonged to Saul.

King David kept his vow and helped Mephibosheth a second time. King David saved Mephibosheth's life in II Samuel 21:5-6. One day, King David prayed about a famine Israel experienced for three years. The Lord answered and revealed to King David the famine was a result of King Saul's plan to annihilate the Gibeonites. King David went to reconcile with the Gibeonites; however they did not have possessions and land in mind. The Gibeonites wanted to even the score when King Saul in his contemplation for Israel and Judah had tried to annihilate all of them. The Gibeonites that survived wanted avenge for King Saul's behavior that killed their loved ones. They asked for seven of King Saul's men to be given to them. King David kept his vow and spared Mephibosheth's life and surrendered seven of Saul's sons. In the plans God has for you, it is important to be responsible in your assignment. The decisions you make today can have an impact on the survivors and next generation.

You are royal according to 1 Peter 2:9. Your situation is not dead, because God is not finished with you. Mephibosheth was brought before David. The king explained that it was his desire to exercise loving-kindness toward Mephibosheth by returning to him "all the field of Saul." Mephibosheth, thereafter resided in Jerusalem and constantly ate at the table of the king.

Today, show kindness to someone and help position him or her into his or her seat in their Jeremiah 29:11 assignments. You have a responsibility to be your brother's keeper. Help your brother or another man experiencing hardships. You are designed and created to be a blessing to others, and do what is right. Be a champion by remembering the vows you made and helping somebody stand on his or her feet. Most of all, be your brother's keeper to maintain the legacy of their father and the Heavenly Father.

Still Point Moment: As you cultivate your ground in the plans God has for you, position yourself to be a blessings. *Psalm 1:2 But they delight in doing everything the Lord wants; day and night they think about his law. (3) They are like trees planted along the riverbank, bearing fruit each season without fail. Their leaves never wither, and in all they do, they prosper.* Get planted to bear the fruit! Get planted, so you won't miss another season. Get planted to bear the fruit. Remember your gifts are designed to bless others stand on their feet. Continue to seek God in prayer more!

Still Transition Affirmations: God's power works best in my weakness! *"My gracious favor is all you need. My power words best in your weakness." (2 Corinthians 12:9a).*

God's Plan for Man: Grieve

Consequences are given as a result of not obeying God or operating below your Jeremiah 29:11 assignments. The results of consequences are the loss of titles and the plan not working. Obedience is written in the Jeremiah 29:11 plans for you. This section is written for you to repent when you are out of line in your assignment. Be encouraged as you read this section to grieve any loss you've experienced. It takes the principles of commitment and responsibly to work in your Jeremiah 29:11 assignments. The objective is to know that your faith has an assignment. As you continue to read, be still as you discover your Jeremiah 29:11 identities.

Still Point: *O Lord, I have come to you for protection; don't let me be put to shame. Rescue me, for you always do what is right (Psalm 31:1).*

"I Will Go to Him One Day (I Samuel 12:23)."

Life and death of friends and family are part of the plans God has for you. It is important to share memories of people and comfort closer relatives. Bathsheba and David's relationship began while she was still married to another man. The result of their coming together was adultery, murder, and death.

At the time of Bathsheba slept with David, she was the wife of Uriah the Hittie. Later, (II Samuel 11:5) when Bathsheba discovered that she was pregnant, she sent a message to inform David. (II Samuel 11:26) When Bathsheba heard that her husband was dead, she mourned for him. (27) When the period of mourning was over, David sent for her and brought her to the palace, and she became one of his wives. Then she gave birth to a son. But the Lord was very displeased with what David had done. (II Samuel 12:1-6) So the Lord sent Nathan the prophet to tell David a story. (7) Then Nathan said to David, "You are that man! The Lord, the God of Israel, says, "I anointed you king of Israel and saved you from the power of Saul. (8)

I gave you his house and his wives and the kingdoms of Israel and Judah. And if that had not been enough, I would have given you much, much more. (9) Why, then, have you despised the word of the Lord and done this horrible deed? For you have murdered Uriah and stolen his wife. (10) From this time on, the sword will be a constant threat to your family, because you have despised me by taking Uriah's wife to be your own, (11) "Because of what you have done, I, the Lord, will cause your own household to rebel against you. I will give your wives to another man, and he will go to bed with them in public views. (12) You did it secretly, but I will do this to you openly in the sight of all Israel. "(13) Then David confessed to Nathan, "I have sinned against the Lord." Nathan replied, "Yes, but the Lord has forgiven you and you won't die for this sin. (14) But you have given the enemies of the Lord great opportunity to despise and blaspheme him, so your child will die."

The ministry of fatherhood is understanding your responsibility to teach and provide for your children. David made mistakes in his position as king. He committed adultery with Bathsheba, plotted Uriah's death, and did not repent for a period of time to God. This cover-up was not the standard of a king. Don't let your lust control you with a daily habit. Live up to your responsibility and hold yourself to a standard of a king. It is your responsibility to pray.

David prayed for a turnaround in the situation, but the baby died. Sometimes, you just have to go through the experience to mature in the Lord and let God have His way. Don't be blind or cover up your involvement in your situation. Any mistakes can be confessed to God. We cannot go on with our lives and avoid responsibility because it can develop into an unhealthy pattern. Denial of your sins and actions can create wedge between you and God. No one can hide from God. David had opportunities where he could have confess to God about the plot and murder of Uriah. However, denial and pride kept him from doing so.

God sent the Prophet Nathan to David to reveal what was to come of the conceived baby. David was willing to listen to Nathan and was able to confess that he sinned against God. For almost a year, David avoided the feelings of conviction which lead to repentance. Nathan's role as a prophet was to be a messenger for God. Thank God for the messengers who are obedient to their callings.

After Nathan returned to his home, the Lord made Bathsheba's baby deathly ill (II Samuel 12:15). (16) David begged God to spare the child; He went without food and lay all night on the bare ground. (17) The leaders of the nation pleaded with him to get up and eat with them, but he refused. (18) Then on the seventh day the baby died. David's advisers were afraid to tell him. "He was so broken up about the baby being sick," they said. "What will he do to himself when we tell him the child is dead?" (19) But when David saw them whispering, he realized what had happened. "Is the baby dead?" he asked. "Yes," they replied, (20) Then David got up from the ground, washed himself, put on lotions, and changed his clothes, Then he went to the Tabernacle and worshiped the Lord, After that, he returned to the palace and ate.

It is important to listen to people who are listening to God. God used the Prophet Nathan to bring David a message. The responsibility to feel convicted and repent was left up to David. The scriptures shows us that we have to change our ways and remain in the will of God. Another lesson is that we learn to accept our punishment. Life is a gift from God, and we have to embrace a relationship with God to know our purpose. We have to keep ourselves in check so we are not in lust or taking from someone else. Cultivate your ground as a responsible gardener of the seeds you planted to understand your purpose.

For that reason, accept your weakness and believe that God is stronger and bigger than your problems. Once you've confessed your sins, you have to get back up again to cultivate the ground in your Jeremiah 29:11 plans. Then, you can comfort and encourage another person in a similar situation. Remember, God has plans for good and prosperity in your future. The plans God has for you come with the spirit of "never give up."

David understood his consequences, and remembered his promise. *24) David comforted Bathsheba, his wife, and slept with her. She became pregnant and gave birth to a son, and they named him Solomon, The Lord loved the child (25) and sent a word through Nathan the prophet that his name should be Jedidiah-"beloved of the Lord," because the Lord loved him.*

The Bible doesn't mention funeral arrangements for the baby; however it mentions another birth. God had plans for David and Bathsheba's second son, Solomon. Solomon became David's successor as king over Jerusalem. Let me encourage you to never give up on God as you continue to discover your Jeremiah 29:11 purposes. God will show up in our path with a word.

Don't give up and throw in the towel. You may need to comfort somebody in his or her time of need. Your comfort can encourage and make someone else stronger in his or her "hard times." Encourage yourself in the Word of the Lord. This is why you can't give up. God will put the shattered and hurt pieces back together. Therefore, be encouraged in the plans God has for you. You could never get right with God if you carry on habits that deceive you. God wants you to be in His will. You can repent and turn to God. In the time of wrong, you have time to be forgiven and repent.

Still Point Moment: Take this moment to confess to God. God corrects because He loves you. God wants you to turn to Him because He wants to bless you. This season learn to ask, wait, and receive the Word from the Lord. As a leader, there is a responsibility to ask, wait, and receive from God the Creator. There is a duty not to cover up your mess. Take a moment and think about some if your losses. How did God add to your purpose? Let me encourage you to *seek ye first the Kingdom of God, all these will be added unto you (Matthew 6:33)*. God will add people into your life to keep you, bless you with favor, and you will develop wisdom to stay on your path to purpose.

Still Transition Affirmations: My hope is in Jesus. *Even when I walk through the dark valley of death, I will not be afraid, for you are close beside me. Your rod and your staff protect and comfort me (Psalm 23:4) I don't have fear because God is with me (Psalm 23:4).*

God's Plans for Man: Trust

Your job is to trust God in your situation. Your faith will work when you trust God. Trust and work are written in the Jeremiah 29:11 plans for you. This section is written for you to build your hope and trust in your assignment. Be encouraged as you read this section about "Trust." It takes this principle to work in your Jeremiah 29:11 assignments. The objective is to know that your faith has an assignment. As you continue to read, be still as you discover your Jeremiah 29:11 identities.

Still Point: *He has given me a new song to sing, a hymn of praise to our God. Many will see what he has done and be astounded. They will put their trust in the Lord (Psalm 40:3).*

Follow Your Vision

As you train up your children you have to set an example and be a lead for them to follow. Their gifts rely on men to lead and position them to recognize their dreams and visions. It is your responsibility to teach your children how to pray and recognize God. Therefore, it is important to have good standing relationships with your children and their friends. Some strategies to discover the plans God has for your children is to ask them questions about possible career and education goals. Also, you can to read the Bible with your children and have discussions about the Biblical people's courageous positions. Another strategy is to give them scriptures to remember that will encourage them and their friends in their time of need. Begin a routine that includes prayer and worship for your child to develop a relationship with God. Have your children participate in youth activities so others recognize their abilities that you cannot see. As you begin to recognize your children's gifts and talents help guide and develop them. As a parent, it is important to be sensitive to their interests and opinions that are different from yours. Therefore, ask God to develop you to become your child's best parent, teacher, coach, and friend.

At times, your children may not understand their training and teachings for their Kingdom assignments, but as their father you have to become their biggest fan and supporter. The purpose of training them is to prepare them for their arrival to a new season and to recognize God's voice in a dream or vision.

Solomon was in a dream, but he was talking to God. He compared his understanding to a child. He asked God for wisdom to govern His people. Let's consider Solomon for an example.

That night the Lord appeared to Solomon in a dream, and God said,

"What do you want? Ask and I will give it to you!" 1 King 3:5. (6) Solomon replied, "You were wonderfully kind to my father, David, because he was honest and true and faithful to you. And you have continued the great kindness to him today by giving him a son to succeed him. (7) O Lord my God, now you have made me king instead of my father, David, but I am like a child who doesn't know his way around. (8) And here I am among your own chosen people, a nation so great they are too numerous to count! (9) Give me an understanding mind so that I can govern you people well and now the difference between right and wrong. For who by himself is able to govern this great nation of yours?"

(10) The Lord was pleased with Solomon's reply and was glad that he had asked for wisdom. (11) So God replied, "Because you have asked for wisdom in governing my people and have not asked for a long life or riches for yourself or the death of your enemies. (12) I will give you what you asked for! I will give you a wise and understanding mind such as no else had or ever will have! (13) And I will also give you what you did not ask for, riches and honor! No other king in all the world will be compared to you for the rest of your life! (14) And if you follow me and obey my commands as your father, David, did, I will give you long life."

(15) Then Solomon woke up and realized it had been a dream. He returned to Jerusalem and stood before the Ark of the Lord's covenant, where he sacrificed burnt offerings and peace offerings. Then he invited all his officials to a great banquet.

Solomon made sacrifice of burnt and peace offerings before the Ark of the Covenant. Also, Solomon celebrated with his officials with a banquet. Let me encourage you to ask and believe that it is already done. Have faith and believe the prayers you prayed are manifested. This means that you believe 'it' is already done. Therefore, walk in faith that God has answered your prayers and has turned your situation around.

As a father, you have to train up your children to succeed you just as David positioned Solomon to succeed him. The time you spend studying the Word of God with your children; such as investing time into their gifts and applying faith into their lives will help them discover their Jeremiah 29:11 purposes. Their faith actions can lead them to recognize God's voice and respond to the vision with a wake-up call.

Let's take a look at Solomon's wake-up call actions (I King 3:5-15).
1. Woke up
2. Realized he had an encounter with the Lord
3. Returned to Jerusalem and stood before the Ark of the Lord's covenant
4. Sacrificed burnt offerings and peace offerings
5. Invited officials to a banquet.

Solomon invited the officials to the banquet because to celebrate their new assignments. As God elevates and promotes you, your children's level increases as well. Therefore, your children have to get ready for their new assignments and responsibilities. You can prepare a banquet for your children and their friends to showcase their talents. Most of all, you can prepare and have annual community celebrations of the people working and making a difference in your community. People need a place they can go and be changed instantly in the name of Jesus.

Expensive name brand clothing and materials cannot equip or protect your child from the devil's plan. For what profits a man to gain the world, and lose his soul (Mark 8:36)? Their Jeremiah 29:11 plans, talents, and gifts are more precious than the latest styles in clothes, shoes, telephones, and other material things. Throughout the book of I Kings, Solomon references his father's prayers and praise while praising God. Solomon witnessed his father, King David giving God praise through worship while seeking wisdom and giving thanks. The scriptures said David openly worshipped and praised God. While David openly expressed his love for God in public, this taught Solomon how to pray, fast, and worship while obtaining the kingdom privileges as a prince. How did David develop this love relationship with God? Jesse, David's father, provided him with a field to shepherd the sheep in the pastures. As you continue to seek first the Kingdom of God, be prepared for a wake-up call. Accept your wake-up call with praise and arrange a banquet. God is speaking to you in your visions and dreams. Solomon was conscious during his dream to answer God and ask Him for wisdom. Be a champion and trust God in your wake-up call.

Still Point Moment: When are you going to wake-up and respond to your purposes, dreams, and gifts God gave you? What is God saying to you about your children to succeed you in their future? How is God providing for you to train up your children in the way they should go and not depart from it? In other words, how are you sowing into your child's life? What investments have you made?

Still Transition Affirmations: *"But blessed are those who trust in the Lord and have made the Lord their hope and confidence (Jeremiah 17:7). Trust in the Lord and place my confidence in him so I am very blessed (Jeremiah 17:7).* As you move forward on your Jeremiah 29:11 journey keep in mind these tips for success as they relate to transition: be self-directed, resourceful, and proactive.

Section Five Reflection: The Ministry of Fatherhood

Let me encourage you to wake up. In an instant, your life can be changed like Mephibosheth. You can be moved from a place like Lo-debar to the Kings' palace. Therefore, you need to have hope in your situation. David's relationship with Mephibosheth, Bethsheba, Solomon, and the people of Jerusalem was designed to help those he loved get to their next level. Therefore, you need to pray for your family. Be your brother's keeper by helping others and keeping your promises. Also, when you grieve you can pray and have faith that your prayers will be answered and accept God's will.

It's not about the exterior things around you, but what's inside your heart. His son, Solomon asked God for wisdom. God is the strength of your faith. You can talk to God through prayer and personal relationship about your situations. If there is anything you want, you have to go through Jesus to get to the Father. It's time for you to know your Jeremiah 29:11 plans and purpose for your life. Therefore, be a positive male figure as a brother, uncle, cousin, mentor, teacher, coach, or adviser to help individuals discover their Jeremiah 29:11 purposes.

Section Six:
Delegate Authority

God's Plans for Man: Build and Equip the Next Generation

Keep the victory in mind as you face situations. "Build and Equip the Next Generation" are written in the Jeremiah 29:11 plans for you. This section is written for you to see wealth in your children and the next generation in your assignment. Be encouraged as you read this section about assignment delegation. It takes this principle to work in your Jeremiah 29:11 assignments. The objective is to know that your faith has an assignment. As you continue to read, be still as you discover your Jeremiah 29:11 identities.

Still Point: *I wait quietly before God, for my salvation comes from him (Psalm 62:1). (2) He lone is my rock and my salvation, my fortress where I will never be shaken.*
Let's examine the relationship between Moses and Jethro. Their father and son-in-law relationship reveals that ministry begins in the home. Ministry begins in your house. You have many roles to act out in your house and in your family. Prior to Moses' arrival in Midian, he grew up knowing his Hebrew identity. Moses was raised by his Hebrew-birth mother named Jochebed in his early years. He went to live in the palace with his adoptive mother which was pharaoh's daughter. Moses knew that he was rescued by Pharaoh's daughter and his real-sister, Miriam. Moses' theme of life included being a rescuer.
Many years later, when Moses had grown up, he went out to visit his people, the Israelites, and he saw how hard they were forced to work. During his visit, he saw an Egyptian beating one of the Hebrew slaves (Exodus 2:11). (12) After looking around to make sure no one was watching, Moses killed the Egyptian and buried him in the sand. (13) The next day, as Moses was out visiting his people again, he saw two Hebrew men fighting. "What are you doing, hitting your neighbor like that?" Moses said to the one in the wrong. (14) "Who do you think you are?" the man replied. "Who appointed you to be

our prince and judge?" Do you plan to kill me as you killed that Egyptian yesterday?" Moses was badly frightened because he realized that everyone knew what he had done. (15) And sure enough, when Pharaoh heard about it, he gave orders to have Moses arrested and killed. But Moses fled from Pharaoh and escaped to the land of Midian.

As Moses grew into a man, he explored the outer areas of the palace. One day as an adult, Moses decided to step out of the palace to visit his people. The Egyptians knew Moses as a prince. However, the Hebrews knew Moses as one of their own. While Moses walked and observed the Hebrew's struggles, he could not withhold back and tolerate the injustice witnessed. On two occasions, Moses intervened to the aid of the Israelites. In the first case, Moses killed an Egyptian soldier beating a Hebrew worker. In the second case, Moses intervened in a situation between two Hebrews. The Hebrew in the wrong said to Moses, *Exodus 2:(14) "Who do you think you are?" the man replied. "Who appointed you to be our prince and judge?" Do you plan to kill me as you killed that Egyptian yesterday?" Moses was badly frightened because he realized that everyone knew what he had done.*

Moses was preordained to be Israelites prince and judge; however it was not his time. Moses' gifts and talents were stirred as he was lead to explore and help his people. His awareness of his identity, gifts, and talents led him to discover his Jeremiah 29:11 plans and purposes. Moses responded to his second case with fright and flight instincts by fleeing. Can you imagine Moses running for his life through the desert? Picture him running and praying for a place to rest, and then he saw a well. A lesson you can learn from Moses is that you have to rest in order to know what direction to go.

He ran until he saw a place to rest. In the moment rest, a situation of injustice took place. Moses observed the situation and could not ignore the injustice taking place against the women. In this third recuse, Moses came to the aid of women drawing water from a well. Even though Moses was exhausted from his journey from fleeing Egypt, he paced over to rescue the women. Be encouraged and continue to operate in your gifts just as Moses did. Moses didn't walk away or ignore the women in need for help. Moses came to the aid of women and rescued them from harassing shepherds (Exodus 2:17). After he rescued the women, then he drew them up water from the well. The report of the rescue was reported to Jethro, the father of these women (Exodus 2:18-19). Then Jethro sent Moses an invitation to their home for dinner. This dinner invitation became a permeant safe haven for Moses. During this time, Moses married one of Jethro's daughters. Yet did Moses realize that he arrived in a safe haven that would prepare him to become an answered prayer and deliver Israel out of Egypt.

In the house of Jethro, Moses had to submit to his father-in-law because he was the covering and head of the household. During this submission, Moses grew spiritually for his purpose. Jethro gave Moses the assignment to be a shepherd. Earlier, Moses learned how to listen to instructions from his superiors: the Pharaoh, Ramses, Jethro, and his birth and adoptive mothers. Let this section encourage you to complete the assignments, goals, and tasks that you've started discovering your Jeremiah 29:11 identity and purpose to build your relationships with others and the people in your home. Submitting is part of the Jeremiah 29:11 plans God has for you. This means to put your agenda aside and do God's purpose. Moses worked in Jethro's house and carried our duties of a shepherd.

God will put people in your life to rescue you from your oppressors. In this text, oppressors can include people and institutional systems that oppress individuals because of their backgrounds. There are lawyers, doctors, teachers, preachers, or people that want to help you become a champion. Therefore, understand that you have to be a champion because you have a victory written in the Jeremiah 29:11 plans for you. This means you need to share your testimony about God healing and deliverance. Also, you may have to go back and rescue, and encourage others in situations you have championed. You are a walking verification of divine transformation when you return to the places and people of your past.

My friends please don't hide or keep your blessings to yourself when God blesses or turns your situation around. Rejoice about it and tell others about God's goodness. If God healed you in your body, you could volunteer in the hospital or nursing home. If you had an addiction to medication or illegal substances, you can support a recovery group or begin a ministry for the family members psychologically affected by co-dependency and anger issues. Your gifts and talents have a purpose through opportunities and invitations. Therefore, in your Jeremiah 29:11 purpose God my send you back to the place you ran from or were humiliated. God will speak to you, give you instructions, and be strong where you are week in your Jeremiah 29:11 assignments.

Steps to Prepare for Your Assignment.

One day Moses was tending the flocks of his father-in-law, Jethro, the priest of Midian, and he went deep into the wilderness near Sanai, the mountain of God (Exodus 3:1). (2) Suddenly, the angel of the Lord appeared to him as a blazing fire in a bush. Moses was amazed because the bush was engulfed in flames, but it didn't burn up. (3) "Amazing!" Moses said to himself. "Why isn't that bush burning up?" I must go over to see this." (4) "Here I am!" Moses replied. (5) "Do not come any closer," God told him. "Take off your sandals, for you are standing on holy ground." (6) Then he said, "I am the God of your ancestors-the God of Abraham, Isaac, and Jacob."

When Moses heard this, he hid his face in his hands because he was afraid to look at God. (7) Then the Lord told him, "You can be sure I have seen the misery of my people in Egypt. I have heard their cries for deliverance from their harsh slave drivers. Yes, I am aware of the suffering. (8) So I have come to rescue them from the Egyptians and lead them out of Egypt into their own good and spacious land. It is a land flowing with milk and honey-the land where the Canaanites, Hittites, Amorites, Perizzites, Hivites, and Jebusites live. (9) The cries of the people of Israel have reached me, and I have seen how the Egyptians have oppressed them with heavy tasks. (10) Now go, for I am sending you to Pharaoh. You will lead my people, the Israelites, out of Egypt.

Moses' Path

Jethro gave Moses an assignment to tend to the sheep. One day, Moses was working in the valley of Sanai when he heard God speak. First, it is important to recognize your environment and discern people's intensions. God spoke to Moses in the form of the burning bush in the valley Sanai. Sanai had an important purpose, which was transforming the people of God's purpose. The burning bush got Moses' attention and then God spoke to him saying, *(Exodus 3:5) "Do not come any closer," God told him. "Take off your sandals, for you are standing on holy ground." (6) Then he said, "I am the God of your ancestors-the God of Abraham, Isaac, and Jacob."* God's intensions were not to scare Moses but to get his attention. From this scripture, God is Holy and where His presence is the ground becomes Holy. Therefore, the ground became consecrated; and Moses could neither stand on nor come close to God's presence in an ordinary manner. In this submission, God gave Moses his assignment.

Moses' immediate reaction to the burning bush was to worship in the presence of God. Second, when you worship you have to lose you/your self-identity in order for God to use you. God told Moses, *"Take off your sandals, for you are standing on holy ground (Exodus 3:5b)."* Moses was instructed to take his sandals off. God gave Moses instructions how to use his hands (Exodus 4:2b) and how to use what was in his hands (Exodus 4:6).

Also, God said, *"I will help you speak well, and I will tell you what to say (Exodus 4:12)." Then God sent, Aaron the Levite, to Moses to be his spokesperson to the people and you will be as God to him, telling him what to say (Exodus 4:16). (17) And be sure to take your shepherd's staff along so you can perform the miraculous signs I have shown you." Exodus 4:20 So Moses took his wife and sons, put them on a donkey, and headed back to the land of Egypt. In his hand he carried the staff of God.*

Third, understand that God is stronger where you are weak. For example, God told Moses, "I will help you speak well." Also, "I will tell you what to say." God will help you complete the Jeremiah 29:11 plans for you. God told Moses that He will be with him. Additionally, God sent Aaron to begin the new assignment with

Moses. In the plans God has for you, God will be strong where you are weak. Let me encourage you to allow God to use you. Therefore, you need to make room for the Holy Spirit to move through you. When God speaks to you, He gives clear instructions about what to say, how to use your hands, and provides help to get to the destination.

Then Moses went back home and talked his encounter over with Jethro, his father-in-law. *"With your permission,"* Moses said, *"I would like to go back to Egypt to visit my family. I don't even know whether they are still alive."* *"Go with my blessing,"* Jethro replied. This interaction between Moses and Jethro demonstrated the relationship and respect between these two men. Therefore, it is important to submit to God to receive what you are expecting. Moses needed Jethro to release him from his duties as a shepherd. Jethro had to find a replacement to continue the work and harvest with other business shepherds in those regions. These work ethics are principles to finish the job and meet appointments.

Making arrangements is important in the plans God has for you. The forms of agreements are important. In addition, this maturity shows growth in Moses because he fled out of Egypt because of fear.   I can imagine Moses remembering his old life in Egypt. While living in the palace, Moses was aware of his Hebrew identity under the Pharaoh's leadership. Moses left Egypt because he was frightened that everyone knew that he had killed an Egyptian and buried him in the sand (Exodus 2:11-16). At this point, Moses became a fugitive in the Egyptian system, and a hero to the Israelites. This time, Moses left Midian with a blessing from Jethro and his family. Therefore, God can transform you and give you favor in your Jeremiah 29:11 assignments.

God can transform you and give you favor with people. Your past is part of the plans God has you. You may be assigned and returned to the people of your past. God will use you to be the answer to the prayer of somebody because you are stronger, wiser, and have a new revelation. Therefore, you cannot be afraid to return where you came from or to the places God want to send you.

There are people who are depending on and waiting for your gift to get them out of Egypt (the place they are suck) and their misery. *Exodus 3:7 Then the Lord told him, "You can be sure I have seen the misery of my people in Egypt. I have heard their cries for deliverance from their harsh slave drivers. Yes, I am aware of the suffering. (8) So I have come to rescue them from the Egyptians and lead them out of Egypt into their own good and spacious land.* God heard the cries of his children, and Moses was the answered prayer for the Israelites. Recognize the gift God has given you. Your gift was designed to bless others. Aaron was waiting for Moses.

God will assign people to develop your skills, talents, and gifts. Therefore, pay attention to those developing you into your gifts. Always pay attention to the people in your path and those who give you assignments. Jethro was Moses' father-in-law, a priest, and a shepherd. Jethro was the head and covering of the household. He taught Moses how to be a shepherd; and how to care and look after sheep. The sheep symbolizes the children of Israel. Moses learned how to care, feed, and have patience with the sheep. Jethro gave Moses his blessing and covering to return to Egypt (Exodus 4:20). However, *before Moses left Midian, the Lord said to him, "Do not be afraid to return to Egypt, for all those who wanted to kill you are dead (Exodus 4:19)."* Moses had nothing to fear upon his return to Egypt. God gave Moses instructions as to what to say to Pharaoh and the Israelites. Also, God gave Moses instructions as to what to do, say with his mouth, use his hands, and the shepherd's staff.

Are you willing to take your shoes off and step into the God's plans for you? Look at your hands? What is God telling you to do with them? What assignments are you giving your children to develop them into their gifts? What talents do you see in them? Jethro and Moses had a unique relationship. Jethro gave Moses his blessing for his assignment.

After the children of Israel stepped out of the dry banks of the Red Sea, Moses began to pastor this generation. Moses had many roles as the leader of this saved generation. People from this region heard about the nation of Israel's victory against the Egyptians. This new reputation led to Jethro visiting Moses.

(Exodus 18:5) Jethro now came to visit Moses, and he brought Moses' wife and two sons with him. They arrived while Moses and the people were camped near the mountain of God. (6) Moses was told, "Jethro, your father-in-law, has come to visit you. Your wife and your

two sons are with him." (7) So Moses went out to meet his father-in-law. He bowed to him respectfully and greeted him warmly. They asked about each other's health and then went to Moses' tent to talk further. (8) Moses told his father-in-law about everything the Lord had done to rescue Israel from Pharaoh and the Egyptians. He also told him about the problems they had faced along the way and how the Lord had delivered his people from all their troubles. (9) Jethro was delighted when he heard about all that the Lord had done for Israel as he brought them out of Egypt.

During this visit, Jethro watched and observed Moses interaction with the people of Israel. Jethro, tells Moses,
"This is not good!" (18) You're going to wear yourself out and the people too. This job is too heavy a burden for you to handle all by yourself. (19) Now let me give you a word of advice, and may God be with you. You should continue to be the people's representative before God, bringing Him their questions to be decided. (20) You should tell them God's decisions; teach how to conduct their lives. (Exodus 18:24) Moses listened to his father-in-law's advice and followed his suggestions. (Exodus 18:27) Soon after this, Moses said good-bye to his father-in-law, who returned to his own land.

God prepares people to meet you. Jethro's advice to Moses was to teach the Israelites how to conduct their lives. The Lord will provide you with wisdom when you move in your divine assignment. Jethro's wisdom to Moses led him to begin delegating authority to the people. In his delegation, Moses began to appoint leaders. These leaders had a responsibility to manage themselves and other people. Also, these leaders had duties and authority they had to commit and serve. Can you imagine Moses conducting the training class, 'How to Conduct Your Lives,' to his newly appointed leaders? Theses trainings classes could have been held weekly, biweekly, or monthly. I can imagine Joshua and Caleb assisting Moses in these training classes.
On both sides of Sanai, Jethro offered advice to Moses. Moses was obedient to his elder. God gave direction and protection to the church of the Israelites in the wilderness. Moses' position to

surrender and be obedient to Jethro is an example of divine wisdom. Like Moses, you have to learn how to face your situations. Most of all, you have to learn to take our shoes off! The lessons learned from the phenomenal relationship between Moses and Jethro helped Moses continue to lead the nation of Israel out of Egypt.

Take a moment to reflect upon the people in your life giving you a word of advice. Throughout the Old Testaments, rocks were used as the foundation place where Abraham, Isaac, and Jacob built wells and alters. The wells and alters were places where God met them and provided them revelations about their Jeremiah 29:11 assignments.

Jesus is the Rock of all ages. Today, you will begin to stand on the Rock of Salvation. As you stand on His rock, you can only go higher from here! A rock was carved and used as a tomb where Jesus' body once laid. This rock was used as an open door. Jesus is the way, the truth, and the light. Jesus is the door, key, and rock in the plans God has for you. Put your faith in Jesus, and you will get to your destiny! There are going to be people in your life that know the Heavenly Father and will advise you in your Jeremiah 29:11 assignments and plans for you and your family.

Still Point Moment: Identify the person who God has placed to be a Jethro in your life. How has this person been a blessing to your life, and your children's life? As a father, you can avoid work overload by delegating house responsibilities to your children. Also, as an entrepreneur you can delegate training opportunities for your children or community members to learn and operate a business. This season, take wisdom from wise people to understand your Jeremiah 29:11 assignments.

Still Transition Affirmations: I am being transformed by God's Word and truth. *My prayer for all of them is that they will be one, just as you and I are one, Father-that just as you are in me and I am in you, so they will be in us, and the world will believe you sent me (John 17:22).*

Section Six Reflection: Delegate Authority

Align yourself within the Word of God as you grow and mature into your Jeremiah 29:11 assignments. Pray and cover yourselves and family with prayer as you leave familiar surroundings and people. The lessons you can learn from the relationship between Jethro and Moses include:

1. Do not overwhelm yourself with work and people's problems.
2. Do not lose sight of the Jeremiah 29:11 plans with overload of work.
3. You have to delegate authority by appointing a partner or helper.
4. Be a servant of the Lord by taking care of God's house and people with assignments.
5. Have the right motives to help somebody's ministry.

You can build and equip the next generation by having positive relations with people in your family, community, church, and business contacts. Your gifts and talents are on duty as you have a regular day. Always be ready to help people in your path when they ask questions. Your answer could help them discover their Jeremiah 29:11 purposes. God will put people in your path for a season to help them get through devastations and betrayals; especially if you overcame similar obstacles.

Like Moses, you will have a field assignment. Your field assignment and experience will help you to grow and mature spiritually for your greater assignment and purpose. While you are in your field assignment, your skills to communicate, have patience for others, and perform duties will develop. Therefore, your spiritual maturity and skills will develop as you experience life lessons.

There is an appointed time for your Jeremiah 29:11 purpose to be revealed to people. Thus, there is a time when your gifts and talents are to be revealed in your purpose time. You may experience resistance from people that know you now or knew you from your past. They may not recognize the newer and maturer you because they are stuck in their own past. Therefore, it is important to be patient with people not aware of their Jeremiah 29:11 assignments and purposes. You need to be understanding and patient with those individuals until they have their wake-up call. In the meantime, make sure do not get overwhelmed or lose sight of your Jeremiah 29:11 plans with work overload.

Lastly, let me encourage you to keep wise people around you with Psalm 1 gifts who meditate on God's Word day and night and does not listen to ungodly council. Also, operate in the Galatians 5:22-23 fruit of the sprits while remaining and abiding in God's vineyard according to John 15:1-27. Continue to walk as a champion in the Jeremiah 29:11 plans God has for you.

Be a champion like:

Adam- Commit to Your Assignment

Jesus- Be Responsible

The Disciples- Follow Jesus

Simone of Cyrene- Know your Purpose

Solomon- Know and Recognize Your Season

The Deer- Be Teachable

Zechariah-Believe

Jacob- Forgive

Moses- Be Head of Your Generation

David- Be Champions

Jesse- Know Your Father

Jonathan-Be Your Brother's Keeper

David- Grieve

Solomon- Trust

Jethro and Moses-Build and Equip the Next Generations

Conclusion

Did you draw meaningful connections with the content? What did you learn, and how will you use this information later to align in your Jeremiah 29:11 assignment? In the meantime learn to wait on your promise by reading the Word of God. The Word of God will tell you what to do next if you be still.

As you prepare the next generation

- Do not forget you have a promise. Look at the next generation with an end view.
- Don't let other people take advantage of your promise.
- Be careful of who you yoke with.

Understand your priorities
- Follow Jesus in your Jeremiah 29:11 assignment.
- Set both short and long-term goals.
- Create effective schedules to pray, study, and attend church.

Be Resourceful
- Take time to learn about Biblical people who were transformed. Use resources to increase your understanding through self and group Bible study.
- Learn to communicate, write, or journal still transition scriptures for your moments to be still.

Be Proactive
- Look ahead at assignments, "*I put my hope in God (Psalm 42:5).*"
- Schedule time to work on major goals and projects early.
- Reward yourself for meeting your goals along the way.

References:

Beers, G., Beers, R., & Tyndale House Publishers (1996). *Touchpoint Bible: God's Word at Your Point of Need (New Living Translation).* Tyndale House Publishing.

Brown, B. (2017). *The Plans I Have For You, Woman: Walk in Victory! (2nd Edition)* Dr. Brandi Brown.

About the Editor

Courtney Berry is the owner and editor-in-chief of Iron PROOF Editing Firm, a professional writing, editing, and proofreading company based in Washington, DC. IPEF offers a range of editorial services to businesses, students, authors, and other individuals seeking to sharpen their writing.

Prior to launching Iron PROOF, Courtney was a public school educator for over a decade and taught reading, writing, public speaking, middle school language arts, high school English, and English as a Second Language (ESL). Musically gifted, when not editing, she spends time composing choral music. She holds professional memberships in the Editorial Freelancers Association (EFA) and the American Copy Editors Society (ACS).

About the Author

Dr. Brandi Brown is the mother of three children, Carandus, Jr., Jamaia, and Imani. Her children are the inspiration of writing and completing the books, *Jeremiah 29:11 The Plans I Have for You, Woman: Walk in Victory!*; *Jeremiah 29:11 The Plans I Have for You, Man: Be Champions!*; *Jeremiah 29:11 The Plans I Have for You, Children and Families: Preparing the Next Generations!*

Dr. Brandi DeShawn Brown is an educator trainer and mentor of School Street-School Counseling and Consulting Services. School Street-School Counseling and Consulting Services offers: college and career awareness workshops, race-relations presentations, and multicultural arts and mentoring designed for students, educators, and individuals and group sessions.

www.ingramcontent.com/pod-product-compliance
Lightning Source LLC
Chambersburg PA
CBHW032142040426
42449CB00005B/360